T5-CQA-927

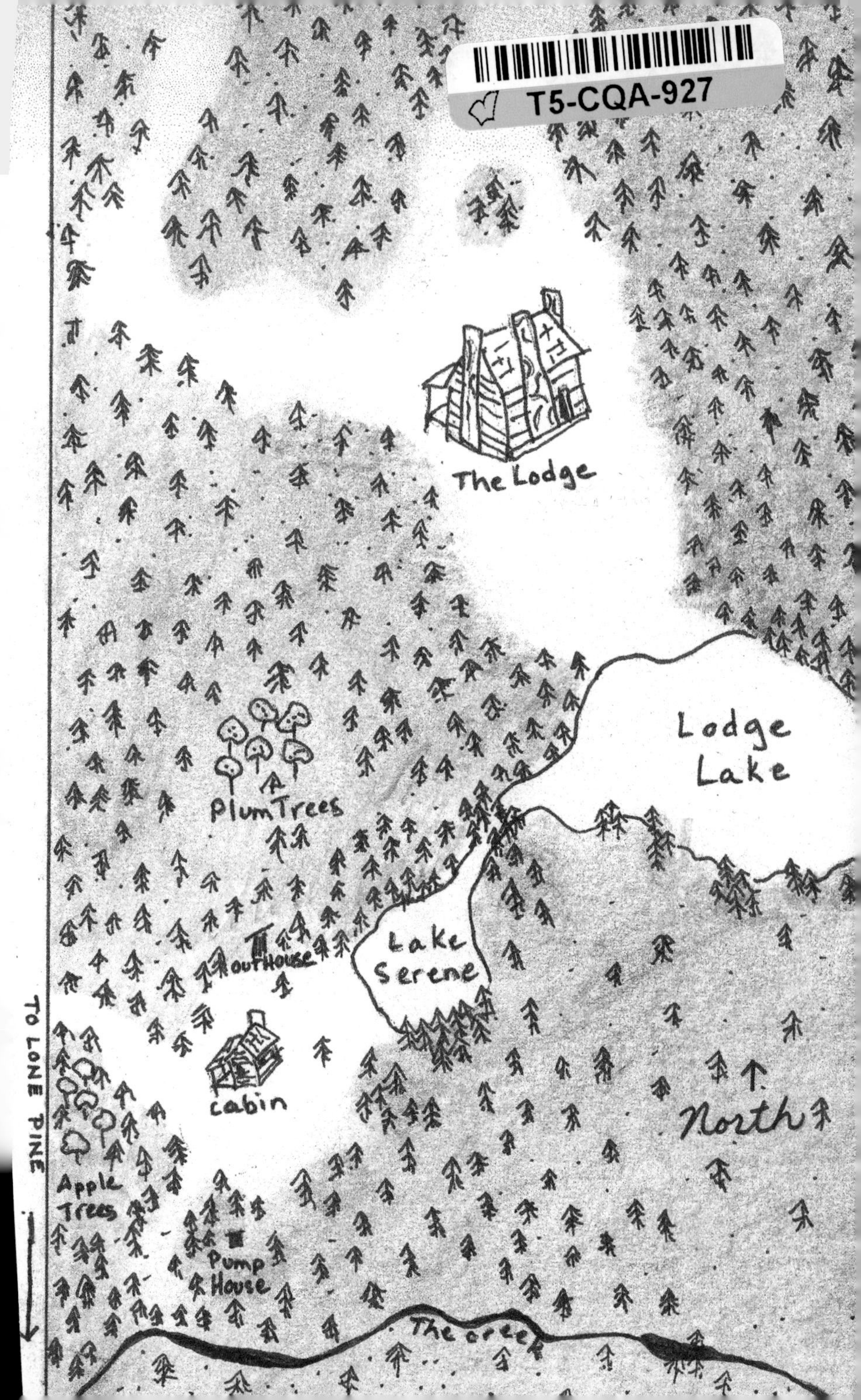

The Lodge

Lodge Lake

Plum Trees

Outhouse

Lake Serene

North

cabin

Apple Trees

Pump House

To Lone Pine

The creek

HOME FIRE

SARAH AND CHARLIE

HOME FIRE

SARAH AND CHARLIE

Nancy Ann

NANCY ANN

IrisBlu
publishing
Tucson, Arizona
IrisBluPublishing.com

For information, please contact IrisBlu Publishing, www.IrisBluPublishing.com.

This book is a work of fiction. Names, characters, places and incidents are products of the author's imagination or are used fictitiously. Any resemblance to actual events or locales or persons, alive or deceased, is entirely incidental.

First printing 2012

ISBN 978-0-9843406-2-0

Dedication

For my children, without whom I would not have had the appropriate insight to write this story; as it is only by experiencing first-hand the love, compassion, happiness, and pride that a child can give its mother did I feel confident about putting these emotions to paper.

For my husband, Tom, who has been ever so patient every time I told him I was "Working on my book!" And who has never deterred me from pursuing this longtime dream that I've had.

To my parents, who after raising eleven children, are prime examples of love, sacrifice, dedication, and faith.

Thank you to the handful of those

who were willing to read

my manuscript in its raw form.

Your encouragement and input is

appreciated.

Especially to Mary Farias.

PROLOGUE

It was the spring 1963. A time when living loose, spreading peace and love was quickly becoming the fashion. Freshly graduated, Joan had planned to increase her hours at work, buy a car, and begin college in the fall. Then she met Larry.

Larry was a thrill-seeking, live-on-the-edge sort of guy. Completely different than any of the other boys Joan had dated. A date with Larry was never dinner and a movie. It was a party on the beach or a road trip with no particular destination.

Each day was new and exciting. He had no schedule to keep. He was his own boss. By July of that summer Joan had begun to stay out all night with Larry, who really had no home, but lived with friends in a crowded house. By August, she just quit going home.

It was mid-September when she woke up to shouting voices coming from the kitchen. The owner of the property wanted everybody out. The rent was three months behind and he wasn't interested in renting to a bunch of hippies any longer. Larry and Steve were trying to convince the owner to give them until the end of the month to come up with the rent. The owner stood his ground. The guy who had originally rented the house and signed the contract was nowhere to be found; everybody had to leave. And they had to leave that day.

Larry and Steve tried to convince everyone to stay together and find another place to rent. Out of the eleven people living there, only four of them had jobs. Joan was one of those four, and she was barely hanging on to it. Bob, Mike, and Pam were not interested. Coincidentally, these were the other three that had jobs. Pam said she was going to move back home with her parents. Bob and Mike were going to find their own places to rent.

"Larry, I think I should move back home," Joan said quietly.

"Don't worry, Baby, we'll figure something out," Larry said. He turned to the remaining six, "Okay, who knows of somebody that will let us crash for a couple of weeks?"

Joan silently picked up her few belongings and stuffed them into her oversized purse. Her common sense was telling her to go home to her parents, but her heart tugged at her to stay with Larry. It was a decision that would change her life forever.

There were 73 people that lived on a farm that Larry and Steve managed to rent in 1964. Joan had later told her daughter that at first it was a good way to live; everyone pitched in to help pay the rent, buy groceries, and maintain the place. They were one big, happy family. But things changed in the late '70s. Steve had left once the lease was up, leaving him free and clear. This left only Larry on the lease. It was at this point where Larry seemed to deem himself "boss." He assigned chores, dictated who would have outside jobs to bring in money, and who would stay to work on the farm. What once were affordable accommodations had changed into a strict commune. Many of the women had young children and no other place to live. Most of the people working outside the farm were men trying to provide for their families. Larry made it quite difficult for anyone to leave. Joan knew that this was done on purpose yet she remained the silent dutiful "wife" that Larry expected her to be. She was angry at herself for letting things get this far. She planned to leave, but first, she had to see to it that her daughter got out.

IV

1

It was a warm spring morning. Sarah stepped out of the hospital with her newborn son and took a deep breath. After hailing a cab, she opened the car door and fastened the car seat into the backseat of the taxi. She instructed the driver to go to the bus station. Sitting quietly as the cab rolled along the city streets, she looked at her precious bundle. She could not stop smiling.

The cab pulled into the bus station and Sarah paid her fare. The driver retrieved her suitcase from the trunk as Sarah carefully removed the car seat.

The driver thanked her and got back into his car. As the cab drove off, she entered the bus station.

"How much for a one way ticket to New York?" she asked the man at the counter.

"New York City, one hundred and fifty-six dollars," he said, eyeing the young lady and infant before him.

"One, please."

Sarah handed him $160 cash. She took the ticket and walked away. She had no intention of getting on that bus. They'd be looking for her soon, if not already, and she was hoping they would track her to New York. Instead, with her baby and her only possessions in her suitcase on wheels, she walked out to the curb and hailed another taxi. She was tired and needed to rest. She had the driver bring them to a hotel just outside the metropolis.

Sarah checked into the room and gently laid her baby in the center of the bed. She smiled as tears of joy came to her eyes. "He is so beautiful," she thought. After washing up in the bathroom, she climbed into bed with her baby. She held him and watched him as he nursed. She took a moment to just relax without thinking about what lay ahead of her.

She named him Charlie. Charles Thomas Brenny. This was the name she and her mother had chosen for a boy early in her pregnancy. It would hopefully help them to stay in contact. "Brenny" was an old family name, now brought again to the surface. She would miss her mother dearly. Although confident that they would be reunited someday, that someday could be years away. Her mother had planned most of this "escape," as that is what it really was, an escape out of a commune gone cult. She wanted more for her daughter and grandchild.

Sarah could only hope and pray that her mother's plan would work and that she, her mother, would not be linked to Sarah's disappearance. One thing she *did* have in her favor was that she knew the media would not be involved. When Larry caught wind that she was gone, he himself would organize a search for her. He would not want to attract attention to himself or his commune.

Sarah and Charlie spent nearly a week at the hotel. She knew it was time for them to move on. Her mother provided her with $3,000 from funds that she had been saving and hiding from Larry for years with the foresight that it would somehow be needed. Sarah had to spend her money wisely, for she knew it wouldn't last forever. She checked out and headed north in a $400 car she had purchased under the new name her mother had created and changed for her – Sarah Rose Brenny. She drove for nearly six hours, stopping only as needed to feed and change Charlie.

It was beautiful country in northern Minnesota. With its heavy woods and clear lakes, the crisp air smelled amazingly fresh. The winter snow was melting and the earth was warming, giving way to budding trees and hardy plant life. She passed through the small towns that basically thrived only in the summer months when the "lake people" came back each year. The farther north she drove, the more secure she felt.

The driveway was barely noticeable from the road but easily identified by the red ribbon that was tied to a tree, just as described in her directions. Stopping the car, she got out to remove the ribbon before following the narrow drive that led her to a small log cabin. It looked so tiny among the tall trees.

"Well, Charlie, we're home... at least for a while." Leaving Charlie snug in the car, she got out and stepped onto the porch of the cabin. Taking a key out of her pocket, she unlocked the door and slowly pushed it open. It was dark inside, as the shutters were closed. She pulled them open on the window nearest the door only to realize that there were shutters on the outside, as well. She stepped out onto the porch and tugged on the board that held the shutters closed on the first window. It wouldn't budge. The board on the next window had some give, but not enough to allow her to pull it off. Looking around for something that could be used as leverage to pry the board, she picked up a fairly large branch and wedged it between the cabin and the board. She pulled hard and thought she had felt the board move. Repositioning the branch, she pried hard again, only to fall backwards onto the ground as the end of the branch snapped off.

Brushing herself off, she went back to the car. Charlie was sleeping soundly. Pulling the keys from the ignition, she opened the trunk. She hadn't looked in the trunk when she bought the car, but was hoping she at least would find a tire iron. There was one, along with a spare tire and a jack. With the tire iron she went back to the window with the loose board. The tire iron was stronger and narrower than the bulk of the branch. Once the tire iron was positioned between the cabin and the board, the board pried off quite easily. She opened the shutters then went back to the door of the cabin and slowly stepped inside. It was evident by the dust and cobwebs that nobody had been there for a while. It was a very simple, one-room cabin. There was a wood burning stove, a table, two chairs, and a bed in the corner. No running water. No electricity.

Returning outside, she pried off the boards that held the shutters closed on the remaining windows. Thanks to the tire iron, they all came off with moderate ease. She latched them open with the wrought iron hooks that were fastened to the logs of the cabin. When she went back indoors and opened the inside shutters, it was quite a bit brighter, but it was still fairly dim due to the tall pines all around the cabin. Besides, it was approaching four o'clock p.m. in mid-April in Minnesota and the sun was beginning to set.

It was also getting chilly. Sarah checked on Charlie. He was warm in his car seat with his blanket and hat. She gathered up some kindling and dry leaves. Opening the firebox door of the stove, she arranged the leaves and wood on the grate inside. She went back outside and gathered up some larger bits of branches and piled them on the floor near the stove then went back to the car and pulled out the small suitcase. Setting it on the table, she took out a zip lock baggie. In there, she found a box of waterproof matches.

She watched as the leaves began to burn and the small bits of twigs caught fire. Smoke began to fill the cabin. Looking the stove over, she noticed a sort of lever on the stovepipe; she turned it just a little. The smoke seemed to change its course. She turned it a little bit more and the smoke obediently drafted up the flue. Her fire grew as she fed it more dry wood. She went outside and saw the smoke coming out of the chimney. Everything seemed to be in working order and she felt that using the wood stove would be quite similar to the fireplace that had been used at the commune.

Sarah carried Charlie into the cabin. Leaving him nestled in his car seat, she moved the suitcase to the floor and set the car seat on the table. She quickly went outside to gather up even more wood; she wanted enough for the night. Once she was satisfied with the pile of wood, she closed the door.

Taking Charlie out of the car seat, she changed him and then sat in a chair in front of the stove. She relaxed as she watched Charlie nurse. "I love you, Charlie," she whispered and stroked his cheek.

Within a half an hour the heat radiating from the wood stove warmed the cabin. The only light was the glow from the opened front door of the firebox. Working by this soft light, Sarah removed the existing bedding from the bed and covered the mattress with a thin blanket she had in her suitcase. She lifted Charlie from his car seat and laid him on the bed, folding the excess blanket over him. Placing the largest piece of wood on the fire, she closed the wood stove door and climbed into bed with her baby.

The cabin was quite cool in the morning when Sarah crawled out of bed. Leaving Charlie under the warmth of the blanket, she opened the wood stove door and saw just a few burning embers. After adding some leaves and kindling, the fire burned hot again. While the cabin warmed, she sat at the table and began a list of things to get when they made a trip into town. At the top of the list – *food, water, candles...diapers...gas...*the list seemed to be growing faster than she could write. She was now down to about $2,100, give or take, and she needed that money to last her as long as possible.

Sarah's stomach growled as she nibbled on the trail mix she had brought with her and she drank one of her last three bottles of water. Looking around at her simple new home, she realized there were quite a few items that she would need, but because money was so dear, she hated to spend any of it. With a heavy sigh, she looked back at her list and began to cross things off.

She would have to think twice before spending any money. Outside, Sarah took everything out of the car (which wasn't much), and laid it out on the bedding she removed from the bed the night before. The bedding, in its defense, was in pretty good shape. It did need a good washing, though. She took inventory of what she had on hand: nine empty water bottles, a flashlight, a partial book of matches, an ice scraper, and an old wool army blanket that had been covering the backseat.

Returning to the cabin, she took note of what it had to offer: a Dutch oven, though it was in definite need of seasoning; an old plastic bucket; two enamelware plates; and a large box of stick matches. Placing more wood on the fire, Sarah realized that she needed something for cutting wood. She would need a lot of wood to keep them warm through the winter – a lot of wood. She would also need to stock up on food. One good snowfall could keep them cabin bound for weeks.

Sitting in front of the fire with Charlie, she began to organize her thoughts. She made a mental list of all that needed to be done before the snow flew. It seemed odd to think about the upcoming winter in April, but there was so much to be done. And even if she got everything done, it wouldn't be easy. "This is going to be hard," she thought aloud.

Once Charlie finished eating, she changed him and put him in the car. The day looked promising as they pulled out of the woods and onto the dirt road. It only took her 15 minutes to get to town. It was a small town with a gas station, a grocery/hardware store, a church, and a diner.

There were perhaps 20 houses dotting the town. It was quite picturesque with their neat yards, picket fences, and even a small river running along one side where some boys sat on the bank fishing.

Sarah parked in front of the grocery store. When she and Charlie went inside, she felt the stare of the few customers in the store. Lone Pine wasn't really a vacation spot, but more of a place where an occasional traveler would gas up and keep moving. She straightened her back, made eye contact, and smiled politely.

Looking down at her list she quickly realized that this town might not have what she needed. If she were to shop here for stocking up, she'd pay a high price for it. She did, however, manage to tuck a few things into her cart around Charlie and his carrier. A few canned goods, a can opener, and some tin foil were about all she could afford. She knew that she was only buying these items to be polite.

The checkout girl was friendly. She smiled at Charlie. "How old is he?" she asked.

"Four weeks," Sarah lied, banking that this girl wouldn't realize the difference between a one-week-old baby and a four-week-old baby. If anybody were to come looking for her, she thought it might be a good idea to at least put a few weeks on Charlie.

She quickly changed the subject. "Is there a larger town near here?" she asked the clerk.

"If you take County Road twenty-four north, you'll run into Long Creek Falls. They have everything there."

"How far is it?" Sarah asked, handing over a fifty-dollar bill.

"About ten minutes," replied the clerk, giving Sarah her change.

"Thank you very much."

Sarah pushed the cart toward the door. She picked up the carrier with one hand and grabbed the grocery bag with the other. When she started the car, she looked at the fuel gauge. It read about half of a tank. She decided to see what the price of gas was in Long Creek Falls. Here, in Lone Pine, it was $1.12 per gallon. "If it turns out to be cheaper here, I'll fill up on my way back," she thought.

She drove slowly through town, past the diner and the church. There was a sign in the front of the church advertising a rummage sale on May fourth and fifth.

"What is the date today?" she wondered. "Charlie was born on the nineteenth, we stayed at the hotel for six days...so today must be the twenty-sixth or twenty-seventh," she figured aloud.

It was a pleasant drive to Long Creek Falls. The cashier at the grocery store was right; they did have everything there. Everything that Sarah needed, anyway, including a large grocery store, a home improvement center, and a large retail store with general merchandise. There were also restaurants, movie theaters – all sorts of ways to part with your money. She decided to part with some of hers at the home improvement store first. She knew this initial shopping spree was going to be pricey, but she had little choice. Still, she managed to cut back on her list, hoping some of the everyday things would be found at the church's rummage sale.

The gas price was the same as the price in Lone Pine so Sarah filled up the tank before her last stop at the Laundromat to pick up the two loads of laundry she had washed while she ran her errands. Three hours had passed quickly. It was nearly two o'clock and she wanted to get back to the cabin. There was barely room for the laundry in her car, but she did manage to wedge it all into the front seat. On her drive back to Lone Pine, she noticed a small rest area. Actually, it was just a dirt parking lot and one old picnic table. What had caught her eye, however, was an elderly man filling up plastic jugs with water. He had four of them.

Sarah steered her car into the lot. "Carson's Spring," a sign read. She got out of her car and asked the man, "How's the water?"

He looked up, a little startled at first, but then replied, "I've been drinkin' it fer over fifty years. Best water I've ever had. It's hard, though. But I ain't rusted yet!" He laughed as he put the jugs of water in the back of his pickup.

Sarah smiled and waved as he pulled out of the lot, wishing she had brought along her empty water bottles. "Next time," she thought. She did have one bottle in the car, though. She got it and filled it up. She took a drink. It was cold and it had a fresh taste to it, but she wasn't certain it was the best water she ever had. It tasted remarkably similar to any other water that she had ever had. "But this water is free," she said to herself. She took another large drink then topped off her bottle and got back into the car.

Pulling up close to the cabin door, she turned the car off. Charlie was still sleeping, but she knew he'd be waking up soon wanting to eat. Quickly, she began to unload the car and brought her new things into the cabin.

With the car unloaded and Charlie inside, she fired up the stove again. She changed Charlie and sat in front of the stove to feed him. Looking around at the cabin she thought, "If walls could talk."

This was her great-great grandfather's cabin. He had built it in the mid-1800s and this was his land. Though she didn't now exactly where the property lines were, she *did* know that 800 of these acres were his. This property had been handed down generation after generation, and now it was hers. Actually, it was her mother's.

Sarah knew nothing of this place until her mother began to include her in on the plan to get her out of the commune. In fact, she really knew nothing about her blood relatives. Her mother didn't speak much about them and now Sarah understood why. The less Larry knew about Joan's family, the better. He had never asked about her family, and Joan never brought them up. She got occasional updates through her sister, Liz, who wrote to her at a P.O. box that Joan secretly kept. It was Liz who tied the red ribbon to the tree at the end of the driveway.

When it occurred to Sarah just how long her mother had been plotting and scheming to get her out of the commune, tears began to roll down her cheeks. "I miss her, Charlie. I miss her so much already." She kissed her baby on the forehead. Taking a deep breath and straightening her back she said, "Just wait until you meet your grandma!" Although she had no idea of when that day would come.

With fresh linens on the bed, Sarah tucked Charlie in and put more wood on the fire. She began to unpack her purchases, beginning with a can of soup and a two-quart saucepan. While the soup heated, she stacked the other canned goods on one of the two shelves on the wall of the cabin. Beneath the shelf, she lined up four one-gallon jugs of water.

The cabin was very dusty and Sarah wished she had convinced herself to buy a broom. She dusted off what she could with a dry wash cloth then wiped things down with another that she had sparingly dampened with water. Soon, she could hear her soup bubbling. She sat at the table and ate right out of the pan with a wooden spoon.

Her stomach growled in appreciation of the hot meal. She had no problem eating the whole pan of soup then mopping it clean with a slice of bread. "Just as well," she thought. "I have nowhere to store leftovers." As she drank her Carson's Spring water and took a vitamin, she jotted down "cooler" beneath the word "broom" on her wish list.

With yet another moistened washcloth, she wiped the pan and spoon the best she could. She now knew that the bargain 12-pack of washcloths was a good buy on her part.

As she put more wood on the fire, she noticed the orange glow of the western sky. The sun would soon be setting so she quickly went outside to gather additional wood. This time she grabbed a couple of larger branches, and with the pruning saw that she purchased, she cut a neat little stack of wood. The logs were certain to burn longer and hotter than the branches she had been using until now – at least she hoped so.

After she was comfortable with what she thought was perhaps a three- or four-day supply of wood, she focused again on unpacking. Though she had bought several candles, she also bought an oil lamp and some lamp oil. With the lamp assembled and the basin filled, she lit the cotton wick. The lamp lit up the small cabin nicely from the center of the table.

2

Sarah awoke to the merry chatter of birds. Lying in the bed, she tried to count how many different calls she heard. It was difficult to tell, but she guessed at least six. Regardless of the number, it was a pleasant way to wake up. However, she found it to be a very brisk morning once she crawled out from underneath the blanket. She got out of bed and quickly tucked the warm blanket around Charlie.

The fire in the stove had gone completely out. Though she had a nice supply of logs in the cabin, there was no kindling to get the fire started. She slipped on her shoes and opened the door. Everything was covered in frost. She pulled up some dead weeds and leaves, as well as a few small twiggy branches, and brought them into the cabin.

Working by the glow of the oil lamp, Sarah broke the twigs into small pieces. With the washcloth she had used to dust the shelves, she patted them as dry as she could. She then crumpled up the receipts she had acquired and put the driest of the weeds and leaves on top of them in the firebox. Striking a match on the cast iron stove, she brought the burning stick to the paper. It and the grass burned immediately, but the leaves did not. In less than 30 seconds, the receipts and grass were reduced to ashes, leaving only a pile of damp leaves and sticks.

Looking around, she grabbed a paper bag. Inside the bag she had thrown all of the rigid plastic and cardboard that came with some of her purchases. She tore a piece of cardboard into small strips about five inches long and one-half inch wide. Then she took a paper towel and tore that into pieces and crumpled them up a little bit. Carefully making a neat pile with the pieces of paper towel, she arranged the cardboard strips in a sort of pyramid inserting a stick here and there.

Charlie stirred on the bed. Looking over her shoulder she said, "Just a minute, Charlie. Mommy needs to get this fire started."

Sarah took another match and struck it on the stove's surface. The paper towels proved easy to burn – almost too easy. At first, she feared that they would burn before the cardboard had a chance to light. But it did begin to burn on its torn edges where it was thinner. The fire grew as the cardboard burned and the few twigs dried out enough to catch on, as well. Sarah let out a sigh of relief and quickly fed the fire some larger strips of cardboard and more twigs.

By now, Charlie was beginning to fuss. Still, she kept breaking up sticks and building up the fire. It was now beginning to burn hot enough to dry the larger twigs and branches she was putting in the firebox so that they would burn. After about 10 minutes the fire was burning small branches about one inch in diameter. She put several of this size on the fire plus one larger log that was nearly four inches in diameter.

The firebox wasn't very large: about 10 inches wide, 20 inches long and perhaps 10 inches deep. She realized that even though Charlie may sleep through the night at some point, she would be up every few hours during the winter keeping the cabin warm.

She changed Charlie then sat in front of the stove to feed him. The cabin was warming up nicely and the sun was well on its way to brightening the day.

"Today," she told him, "we are going for a walk." She kissed his head gently and held him snuggly as he ate and fell back asleep.

While Charlie napped, Sarah walked around the perimeter of the cabin gathering in her arms each branch and stick she came across. She sat on the porch and broke them into kindling size and laid them in a neat pile near the door. She thought that they would stay dry there. Soon a sizable stockpile of kindling had grown. Next she dragged any large branches, and even a few tree trunks, close to the front of the cabin. Starting the car, she backed it up and parked it about two feet from the porch. She lifted a large branch and laid it across the trunk of the car and porch rail. She began to saw the wood into logs.

After two hours she had a fair amount of wood cut. She looked down at her hands. They were red and sore. She poured some water into her small saucepan and soaked them the best she could. The cool water did help to alleviate the pain, if nothing else.

Sarah and Charlie began their walk around noon. Charlie was content cradled within the sling she had devised out of a sheet. "This is so much easier than lugging around that car seat," she observed. She thought Charlie probably preferred it to the car seat, anyway.

Sarah walked only about 150 feet north of the cabin and made her first discovery. Off to the left was a tiny building tucked among the trees. "So there's the outhouse," she laughed. As she walked toward it she scanned the ground for a large stick. Unsure of what may be inside, she approached the outhouse slowly. With the crooked nook at the end of her stick, she cautiously pulled the door open and waited a moment to see if anything would come out. Keeping the door in front of her, she peeked around it to look inside, prepared to defend herself and her child. Convinced that the outhouse was empty, she relaxed a bit and pulled the door wide open and took a better look. It was just a standard, hole-in-the-bench outhouse.

"Chirp!"

Sarah screamed and jumped back. Dropping her stick she instinctively put her arms around Charlie in his sling. A chipmunk scurried past her and scampered into the woods. Though she could feel her heart pounding inside her chest, she breathed a sigh of relief. "I have got to get a grip if

I am going to be living out here," she said aloud. Disappointed in herself for dropping her only weapon, she picked up her stick again and walked away from the outhouse.

The cabin sat on a hilltop that overlooked a clearing with a small lake at the bottom. The water quietly lapped at the shore. It was very calm with just a few ripples on its surface. Sarah could see from where she stood that it was shallow for at least 20 feet out. "It is way too cold now, but I bet in July we'll be down here a lot, Charlie," she said, patting him through the sling. She walked along the shore's edge for a while but came to a halt where it became swampy. A grove of dried cattails prevented her from wanting to venture farther. It dawned on her that in a couple of months this area would be green and overgrown again with weeds.

Walking back along the shoreline, she looked around the lake. As far as she could tell, there were no cabins, boats, or docks. Nothing that would indicate others living nearby. She wondered if the entire lake was within the property lines.

She began to walk back up the hill to the cabin. This time she walked along the southern edge of the tree line, looking up into the trees, which were primarily pines. Here and there she spotted a birch or an oak. There were others, too, but for the most part, the pines dominated.

The sun shined directly above the cabin and its warmth felt good. Inside the cabin it was noticeably cooler even though the fire was still glowing. The large round log proved to burn quite long but it didn't seem to be putting out a lot of heat. She added some smaller branches and a couple of the one-inch logs to get the fire going again. Just by picking up a log, Sarah was instantly reminded of how sore her hands had gotten. A sinking feeling came over her as she realized just how much wood she was really going to need to cut.

With Charlie still napping in the sling, she decided to check out a path just south of the cabin. It apparently had been worn into the landscape by a vehicle of some kind; there were just two tire tracks that trailed off into the woods. She hadn't walked far when she came to another clearing. Off to one corner of the clearing were the remnants of a small log building. It still had four walls, but no roof and no door. There were a couple of young trees growing inside of it. The sun shining above made the clearing bright and warm. Sarah figured it must have been a pasture once upon a time.

Her mother told her that the cabin had been vacant for several years, and before that it was primarily used in the summer months. Occasionally, it was used in the fall during hunting season. Though her mother hadn't been there since she was in her teens, she had vivid memories of her summers spent at the cabin. As soon as school let out, she and her family would pack up and head for the lake. They spent the entire summer there. Her father would work during the week and join them as soon as he could on Friday afternoons, and sometimes he even took a few days off.

Sarah recalled the look on her mother's face as she reminisced about family vacations and holidays. She knew that her mother missed her family dearly and couldn't imagine what it would be like to be away from her own mom for so long.

"But I guess I am about to find out," she sighed. She knew that her leaving the commune was what her mother really and truly wanted her to do, but each day Sarah was finding herself longing to see her. Suddenly, she felt like she needed a hug, so she hugged Charlie in his sling. "This is all for you, Charlie. You'll get to meet your grandma, I promise. We just have to be strong. And patient."

She walked across the clearing and back into the trees. The fallen trees that littered the ground would eventually become fuel for her fire. She hadn't walked far when the land began to slope downward. Sarah could hear the movement of water. Walking toward the sound, she encountered a creek that was about 12 feet wide. Across the creek Sarah could see there was still snow on the north slope going upwards away from the water.

Carefully reaching out a bit, Sarah poked her walking stick into the water. She pulled it back out and looked at the end. It was wet about two feet up. She wondered how deep this creek would get. Charlie began to wiggle in his sling. He was trying to stretch, but only managed to get one hand out into the fresh air. Sarah started to walk back to the cabin. "I'll bet you're ready for a feed and change, aren't you?"

As she approached the cabin, she stopped in her tracks. From the woods, she noticed that the door was open.

"Did I leave it open?" she wondered. She was certain that she had pulled the door shut. Crouching behind a pine tree as best she could with Charlie in his sling, she scanned the area with her eyes. Her heart began to pound hard in her chest and it was about all she could hear, too. "Please don't let them find me...please don't let them find me..." she pleaded and prayed. Her mind began to race. "They'll take Charlie from me! They'll never let me see Mom! I can't let them find us!"

"Snap!" went a small branch behind her. Her back straightened. Sarah turned her head slowly toward the noise. At first she saw nothing. Then she saw something moving out of the corner of her eye, and she could hear by its footsteps that it was coming closer. Her eyes were open as wide as could be while she tried hard to keep her breathing regular and quiet. The figure came into view. Though Sarah was relieved, she was frozen in awe. A large deer with enormous antlers walked by her only about 20 feet away. It stopped briefly to look at her and Charlie, then let out a snort and trotted off into the woods.

Sarah closed her eyes and gathered her wits. With a deep relaxing breath, she focused again on the cabin. The only car she could see was her own. She couldn't see any figures inside the cabin, though the windows seemed to only allow reflections of the trees outside. She didn't hear any voices, either. She began to doubt herself about closing the door. Perhaps it didn't latch and a breeze blew it open. Still, she waited. Charlie fussed in his sling. Sarah positioned him so he could nurse. This calmed him down as she sat and watched the cabin for another half an hour.

With Charlie sleeping again, she adjusted him comfortably and slowly stood up using her walking stick. She felt confident now that nobody was in the cabin. "How would anybody have found me, anyway?" she reasoned. Only her mother and her mother's sister knew where Sarah was and she knew that neither of them would have revealed her whereabouts to anybody.

Cautiously she approached the cabin, watching with care that she didn't step on any twigs. There weren't many about, as she had gathered nearly all of them in this area for the fire. Still, there were a few freshly fallen ones. Sarah wanted to peek into the window near the bed, so she walked around to the side of the cabin. This gave her full view of the entire one-room home. Stooping just beneath the window, she slowly righted herself and peered through the glass with one eye. She didn't see anybody, but it was obvious that someone or some*thing* had paid a visit while they were out.

She walked all the way around the cabin, peeking into each window. Holding the walking stick tightly in her hand, she was prepared to defend Charlie and herself. "This time I won't drop it," she promised. She pushed the door all the way open. The bags from her shopping trip had been pulled out and scattered about. Three of the many instant soup packets had been torn open and apparently chewed on. The loaf of bread was history. She was thankful that the bulk of the food she bought was canned goods, a tip she'd keep in mind every time she went shopping.

She didn't know for certain what type of critter had been here, however she suspected it was a raccoon. "I thought they were nocturnal..." she mused as she inspected the door latch. It did stick a little bit. She would have to be certain that it latched properly before she left the cabin in the future.

She closed the door and took Charlie out of his sling, changed him, and let him stretch out on the bed. He was content as she fed the fire and cleaned the cabin. To her wish list she added "food locker," which, in her mind, would be a sturdy plastic storage bin of some kind.

The morning was warm when Sarah woke up. "I could get used to this," she thought. She added only enough logs to the fire to enable her to make some oatmeal, as they were going into town early. It was the first day of the rummage sale at the church in Lone Pine and Sarah was hoping to find some useful items at a bargain price. "One man's junk..." she thought.

She gathered up her empty water bottles in a plastic shopping bag and put them in her car. In a larger bag, she had all of the garbage she had accumulated, which was mostly diapers, and placed that bag in the trunk. She also had a few cans to recycle, but would need to find out where to bring those. She wasn't even sure of where she was going to bring her garbage.

Once she pulled out of the woods and onto the dirt road, it was evident that today was going to be a beautiful spring day. She hit "seek" on the car radio until she found a local station that offered news and information. It was already 55 degrees and the weatherman said highs would be in the upper 60s. She welcomed the warmer weather.

The town was busy. As she approached the church, parking became more and more sparse. Sarah drove past the church. She first wanted to fill up her bottles at Carson's Spring and get rid of her garbage, if possible. Before she turned into the parking lot, she was happy to see a large barrel with the word "TRASH" painted on it. She parked her car and removed the bag of garbage from the trunk and dropped it into the barrel. She began to fill up all of her empty water bottles, plus three of the four gallon jugs she had purchased the week before. In the back of her mind she wondered what she would do for water in the winter. The likelihood of getting snowed in was high. She didn't think she'd be able to shovel her way out of the driveway, though she knew she could always park her car out toward the road. "Maybe I should have bought a truck," she thought as she replaced the cap on the last jug of water and carried it back to her car.

Charlie was awake and alert. He looked at Sarah as she leaned into the back seat to set the water down. "I love you, Sweetheart," she cooed to him. Charlie looked back at her lovingly. Sarah kissed him gently on his chubby cheek and said, "Okay, Buddy, let's go find some treasures!"

As she approached the town again, she decided to drive past the church, hoping to get a close parking spot. She knew it was likely that she'd be purchasing several items that she'd need to haul back to her car. There was nothing available in the front of the church. Driving slowly, and yielding for the many pedestrians, she turned to go around the block. There was a large parking lot in the back and she was surprised to see that there was also a school along with the church. She turned into the parking lot at the sign that read "St. Joseph's" and then proceeded to list the times of the church services for Saturday and Sunday.

The parking lot was just as busy as the street that ran through town. Sarah found a parking spot that was relatively close to an entrance that people were coming and going through. Unfastening Charlie from the car seat, she settled him into his homemade sling. His big, dark eyes stared up at Sarah.

She took her cash out of one front pocket of her jeans and pulled out $180, which she put in the opposite front pocket.

The church basement was full of tables of clothing of every size, linens, towels, footwear, dishes, pans… it went on and on. The organization of it all made it easy to shop. She made a beeline for the winter clothing. There she found some ski pants and a parka for herself. The parka was a little big, but would fit nicely over bulky sweaters. She found some warm winter boots. Again, they were a bit too big, but nothing a second pair of socks couldn't fix. She found warm clothing for Charlie also, in several sizes. She gathered it all up in her arms. Alongside the children's clothing, there was everything from cribs to walkers. She saw exactly what she needed. She walked toward the strollers then stopped suddenly. Somebody got to the stroller she was looking at before her and was checking it out.

"This one is only fifteen dollars!" Sarah heard the lady say to her husband as he walked up beside her. They continued to discuss and examine the stroller. Sarah walked around looking at the other baby items, hoping they would leave. They did leave, but they took the stroller with them. Sarah was disappointed as she looked at the three umbrella strollers that were left. Not exactly what she had in mind. The one the couple left with was a large, heavy-duty stroller that could easily be maneuvered outside the cabin. The umbrella strollers were lightweight and didn't look as comfortable. Still, she did grab the one of the three that was just a bit nicer. It had heavier wheels and storage beneath the seat. It also had an awning that offered shade. She thought it was worth the three dollars.

Actually, it was worth the three dollars just to be able to put all of the clothing she had in her arms in it and push it around through the rest of the sale. She saw a lot of things that she wanted to buy. Much of it was clothing, as neither of them had any to speak of, and everything was priced to move. Baby T-shirts were only ten cents each. She felt selfish as she grabbed nearly all of them. The clothes were beginning to fall off of her over-packed stroller. She decided to pay for these items, put them in the car, and then make a second round.

Upon her return to the sale, she first went to the toy section. There was a wagon that had removable sides on it. She knew it would prove to be very handy at the cabin. "At *home*," she said aloud to Charlie. She pulled it from the toys and proceeded to fill it with necessities.

As she paid for her wagon full of goodies, the lady taking the money told her quietly, "You know, tomorrow starting at noon, it's the bag sale. All you can put in a bag for one dollar." Sarah thanked her for the information and told her she'd likely see her tomorrow.

3

By the time they reached the driveway, Charlie was just beginning to fuss. She carried him into the cabin and set him on the table, carrier and all. He "watched" as she built a fire. It felt warmer outside than it did inside the cabin. Sarah hoped this would be true during the hot summer months.

With the fire burning, Sarah changed Charlie then sat in front of the stove to feed him. "You are getting so big so fast," she said softly, holding his tiny hand.

Charlie was soon sound asleep with a belly full of milk. Sarah made herself some soup with crackers for lunch. She didn't find anything she could use to store food in at the rummage sale and decided she'd just have to buy one at the retail price.

She finished her lunch then spread a quilt out on the porch and began to sort through all she had bought. She was very pleased with how much she got for $32.50 and was excited to go back tomorrow for the bag sale. There were many things there that she did not deem as necessities, but at $1 per bag, she could afford them. "If they're still there," she reminded herself.

Sarah stood up and stretched. She leaned against the porch railing and pondered where to put all of this stuff. She had no dresser, and only two shelves. There were three wooden pegs built into the wall of the cabin near the door, but those offered only so much.

She decided to put the baby clothes according to size into some bags she saved from her initial shopping spree and put larger sizes back into the trunk of the car. The blankets and quilt would be folded and sit on the foot of the bed. She hung the ski pants and parka on one of the wooden pegs. Eventually, everything seemed to have found a home. Still, she'd like a dresser to keep things clean and off of the floor. She opened up the stroller and put a large bag of cloth diapers in the seat. She had no pins yet, but would pick those up tomorrow. "I'll need something to wash these in," she thought. The diapers were one of her best finds. She knew they would save her a lot of money.

With everything put away and Charlie sleeping, Sarah decided to cut more wood. She was beginning to hate this chore, mainly because her hands hurt so much. Still, she dragged a large broken limb from the edge of the woods near the cabin and began to saw.

4

Charlie slept for nearly three hours, during which time Sarah cut up three large limbs. One from an oak tree, one from a birch, and she wasn't certain of the other, though she did know it wasn't pine. She also pulled out the deep reservoir pan from the stove, using her new oven mitts! It was in good shape. She wanted to bring it down to the lake to give it a good cleaning. She was excited to have hot water on hand, even if it was only perhaps three to four gallons at a time.

Sarah set the reservoir on the porch to cool down, which wouldn't take long as the temperature was dropping quickly with the setting of the sun. Anticipating a cold night, she grabbed an armload of wood and additional kindling from the porch. Closing the door, she locked it from the inside. She jabbed at the fire with what she referred to as her "poker stick" and added wood to the fire.

The large cook stove heated her humble home very nicely. Though she was concerned about the long Minnesota winter ahead of her, she was confident that if she had enough wood, they would be able to stay warm.

At the table, she sat with pen and paper, appreciating the warm comfort the oil lamp offered. In it's soft glow, she began to write out her game plan. She had not figured that cutting wood was going to be a part of her life until she arrived at the cabin. There was an abundance of fallen trees all around her, but she was beginning to doubt whether she'd be able to keep up with the supply/demand ratio with a pruning saw. She added "chainsaw" to her wish list. Sarah hadn't a clue how much one would cost. Maybe she could find one at a garage sale. With that, she would also need a gas can.

With a chainsaw she'd be able to cut several days worth of wood in just a couple of hours. She also wanted to be able to split the wood. There was a large old stump behind the cabin that had been used for splitting, along with a small pile of wood that had been split already. She found that these split logs burned hotter than whole round logs. However, the round ones did indeed burn longer.

Next, but equally as important, came food. Sarah had never hunted, but she knew how to fish and garden. At the commune, they had an enormous garden every year and they canned all of their produce. She did have a supply of vegetable seeds that she took with her the day she left for the hospital, but she had no canning equipment whatsoever. She had no gardening tools, either, for that matter.

Her wish list was now growing again, faster than she could write. The only reassurance was that she was confident that many items on it were likely to be found at any given garage sale.

Charlie began to cry from the bed. Sarah walked over and picked him up, kissing his soft skin. She changed him and sat down to feed him. With her free hand she continued to work on her game plan. She would definitely need to garden. Things like squash, onions, potatoes, and pumpkins were all good crops to grow, as she would be able to store them for some time through the winter without having to can them. Tomatoes would be great if she had canning jars. She could process those in a hot water bath safely enough. Vegetables such as beans, peas, and corn, however, she'd prefer to use a pressure canner.

A large clearing surrounded the cabin, so she had the space for planting. It would allow her to work nearby while Charlie slept. The ground was just beginning to thaw completely in northern Minnesota. Sarah knew it would be nearly June before the soil would be warm enough for planting. But she could make a jump-start on the season by starting the seeds inside the warm cabin – if there was ample light.

She patted Charlie's back gently until he let out a nice burp. He then wiggled a bit to get comfortable and looked up at his mother. They looked at each other while Sarah sang songs to him. She thought about his father.

Sarah was only about three months pregnant when her husband, Cory, died in a farming accident. He was a good person and the news was devastating. But with tremendous support from her mother and the other women, she was able to move forward. This was when her mother put her longtime plan into action. With Cory gone, there was no reason for her to stay. Now was the time to get her out and into the free world. Her mother was not about to let Sarah make the same mistake that she had made so many years ago. Leaving the commune was not as simple as walking away. At first, it was a choice one could have made, but over the years Larry became more and more controlling.

Her mind turned toward her mother. Was she going through some sort of interrogation? She hoped not. Sarah remembered back to when she was 12 or so years old, somebody left and Larry relentlessly questioned everyone. Perhaps the relationship that her mother had with Larry would allow some leniency. She decided not to dwell on it. Her mother told her not to worry, that everything would work out as she had planned as long as Sarah stuck to her end of it. Sarah promised she would and that was a promise she could not break. She knew her mother had grown to be a strong woman and had faith that they would one day be reunited.

Sarah smiled at Charlie and tucked him into his car seat on the table. She rustled up the hot embers and partially burned logs then added more wood to the fire. She poured some water from one of the gallon jugs into her saucepan and set it on the stove. It didn't take long for it to come to a boil. Adding some oatmeal to the water, she stood and stirred her dinner.

5

Sarah had gotten up every two to three hours to put wood on the fire. She could tell this had been their coolest night thus far. As she walked across the room from the bed to the stove, she felt the cold wind drafting into the cabin. There were areas of the log walls that had lost some of the mud filler that was used to pack the gaps between the logs. "Those will need to be dealt with," she thought as she enjoyed the warm glow of the fire on her face.

She fed the fire and thought of how enjoyable a cup of hot chocolate would be, or tea, or even coffee. A note of that little luxury would be added to her wish list. She closed the upper lid of the firebox and walked over to the window. The bright moon cast a soft light into the cabin and its beam glowed across the lake. It looked like a painting.

The sun would be up soon and she had many things she wanted to get done today. Knowing Charlie would be up in about an hour, she took time to feed herself and organize her day on paper. She would go to Long Creek Falls around ten o'clock a.m. to get groceries, diaper pins, something to use as a food locker, and anything else she knew wouldn't be at the rummage sale. Afterward she'd head back to Lone Pine at noon for the bag sale.

There were many things to do around the cabin, as well, such as cut her daily quota of wood. She needed to figure out where she was going to put her garden. She had some seeds that could go into the ground quite soon, like lettuce, radishes, and carrots. Others would be started indoors then transplanted once the ground warmed up. She ate silently, making her notes.

The sky was crisp and blue when they left for town. The sun shined brightly. Still, the air had a nip to it. Sarah had put a couple of round logs and a large split oak log on the fire before they left, hoping the fire would still be burning to keep the cabin warm by the time they returned.

The main street through Lone Pine was bustling with activity. Sarah steered her way slowly through town and headed for Long Creek Falls. She liked the drive to Long Creek; tall pines divided the highway and there was nothing but the same tall pines on the right side of the road. The air smelled fresh. Every so often there was a dirt road that would lead to the scattered residences and farms. At one point, the trees gave way to a large lake. Sarah spotted a boat floating with a man fishing patiently in it. As she made the bend around the lake and came into town, she saw a sign advertising a neighborhood garage sale. Sarah changed lanes and followed the signs.

She parked her car about a block from where the sales began. With Charlie snuggled into his sling, she grabbed a backpack, which she had purchased at yesterday's rummage sale, and strapped it onto her back.

The first few sales didn't offer her much. They mainly had electrical gadgets or media requiring an electrical gadget. She did pick up a cookbook that covered nearly every topic you could imagine, however. There were ten houses altogether having sales. By the time she went to

49

all ten, she had spent only $19.50 and was very pleased with what she had found.

With her new treasures she continued to head toward Long Creek. She was happy to be able to cross some things off her list that she was about to buy new. Sarah now decided it would be all right for her to splurge on some tea bags and hot chocolate mix.

She stopped at the home improvement store to check the prices of chain saws. They ranged from $125 to over $300. She weighed and considered her options. Buying a new one, she'd at least feel good about its working properly for a long while. However, a used one may work just as well, and at a fraction of the price. She decided to wait and see how much one would go for at a garage sale. If she didn't come across one, she'd just buy new.

She pushed her cart to the storage area of the store. Looking over the containers, she selected two large, heavy-duty bins with lids that latched. She also picked up a pair of nice leather work gloves along with a 3-pack of cotton gloves, a broom, a dustpan, seeds, soil, starter trays, and a large garbage can.

She packed her trunk the best she could but ended up returning to the store to buy some rope to tie her trunk down over the bulky items.

Her next stop was the grocery store. She bought a variety of canned goods, along with baking goods, tea, and a large can of hot chocolate mix. By the time she loaded the groceries into the front seat of the car, Charlie was beginning to cry. She laid him on the back seat and changed his diaper, adding it to her small bag of garbage she brought from home. She bundled him up in a receiving blanket, sat in the back seat of the car and fed him. He ate for about a half an hour, and then Sarah strapped him into his car seat and drove back toward Lone Pine.

She made a stop at Carson's Spring to throw away her garbage and fill her water bottles and jugs before going to St. Joseph's for the rummage sale. It was there that she really got a bang for her buck. She filled four bags full of miscellaneous kitchen utensils, pots, pans, baby clothes, towels, and in one bag by itself, a large quilt.

The last stop out of town was at the little grocery store in Lone Pine. There she bought a gallon of milk, butter, eggs, and two large bags of ice and an ice block. Sarah was giddy with excitement as she drove home. She had spent nearly $200 today, but she felt good about her purchases.

The sky was still bright and clear and the air still chilly when they pulled up to the cabin.

Sarah was happy to see a little bit of smoke rising out of the chimney. She brought Charlie inside and set him on the table. Once the fire was fueled with logs, she again spread her quilt out on the porch. Then she began to unpack her car, beginning with the trunk, so she could get to the cooler she had found at a garage sale. She set it against the cabin on the porch where it would always be in the shade. Placing the block of ice in the center of the cooler, she divided one bag of cubes on either side of it. She quickly saw that she might have too much ice. With the milk and butter in next, she poured what she could of the second bag of cubes in and set the eggs on the top.

There was still about one-third of a bag of ice left. Sarah took a large stock pan from one of her bags and put the remaining ice inside of it. She then shoved a few water bottles into the cubes and covered it with the lid. Next she set the two storage bins side by side on the porch. In one, she placed food items such as flour, sugar, and bread on one side of the bin. On the other side she stacked things like kitchen towels and dish rags. In the second bin, she would store the larger baby clothes she had bought yesterday, along with the large bath towels, then articles of clothing she and Charlie would use on a daily basis. She placed the clothing bin at the foot of the bed. The kitchen bin was put in the corner near the stove, between the two shelves on the wall.

She worked for another half an hour putting things away. The cabin was filling up, and Sarah liked it. She was truly beginning to feel like she could live here.

She poured a gallon of water into her new white enamelware coffee pot. After revving up the fire with her poker stick, she added a piece of oak to it and set the pot on the stovetop. The reservoir still needed to be cleaned and filled. She thought again of how great it was going to be to have hot water on hand!

Before feeding herself, she picked up Charlie from the car seat, where he had fallen asleep. He was still sleeping soundly as she snuggled him in the bed. He'd be waking up soon, wanting to eat. She was glad. She had been so busy with everything that it felt like it had been days since she just sat and held him.

Sarah spent the next couple of weeks working outside as much as she could. Each day she cut her quota of wood. This chore was not as bad as before, now that she had gloves. She also worked up the earth where she would be putting her garden. The soil was quite sandy, which made for easy digging. She wondered how fertile it would be for growing her fruits and vegetables. Her other large concern was water. If Mother Nature didn't provide, she would have to haul water either from the creek or the lake. "At least we have that option, right Charlie?" she said aloud. She smiled at Charlie, who was in his car seat tucked in the wagon with a large quilt around him. The days were still a bit chilly as they were approaching mid-May. But the trees were budding and the leaves grew noticeably larger each day. Sarah enjoyed getting up in the morning to a hot cup of tea or cocoa and listening to the woods around her come alive with the chatter of squirrels and chipmunks, and the pretty songs of the birds.

Charlie usually woke up about an hour after Sarah. Either that, or Sarah woke up an hour before Charlie. The latter was probably more accurate, as she would see to it that the fire was burning hot and the cabin was warm before she pulled Charlie from his snug little nest.

Today they would have to go into town. All but one water bottle was empty and the ice block in the cooler was reduced to about half of its original size. There was a lot of cold water in the cooler, though, which Sarah used for cooking and washing dishes.

She fed herself and Charlie then headed into town. It was a warm day and it felt good to get out. At Carson's Spring, she filled her water jugs and bottles. She threw her garbage out, which was minimal now that she had been using the cloth diapers.

As they headed toward Long Creek Falls, Sarah stopped at two garage sales. At the first, she bought three large boxes of canning jars, another cooler, and a bag of clothespins. The second sale had less to offer, but she did find a splitting maul.

Their first stop in Long Creek Falls was the Laundromat. She put one large load into the washing machine, the bulk of it being diapers. She didn't bother to separate the colors from the whites. She just washed everything at once using a baby detergent. That was good enough for her. For the past couple of weeks she had been washing Charlie's diapers using lake water then rinsing them in hot water that she had heated on the stove. The water in the reservoir did get quite hot, but Sarah preferred to dip the diapers in boiling water for their final rinse. Since they were in town, she decided to give everything a good wash in a machine.

They waited 20 minutes while the laundry was in the washer, then Sarah threw the load into a dryer. While the clothes were drying, she went to the home improvement store. She bought three rolls of chicken wire. She hadn't thought of it until she noticed that some of the peas that sprouted in the garden had been nibbled off. She was hoping this chicken wire would deter the rabbits. However, the deer would definitely pose another problem; they would be able to leap over anything she put up.

Sarah also put a dozen steel fence posts and fasteners in her cart. They were a little expensive, but essential for constructing the fence. In the garden center, they were having a sale on all vegetables and bedding plants. She bought seed potatoes, garlic, and onion sets. She was tempted to buy some strawberries, but deemed them unnecessary. She did allow herself to buy some herbs: chives, sage, oregano, lemon balm, and tarragon.

"How old is your baby?" a woman suddenly asked. She startled Sarah and caught her off guard.

"Excuse me?"

"Your baby. How old?" the woman smiled at Charlie in his sling.

"Oh, he's nearly seven weeks," Sarah lied, maintaining the three-week nudge she had given Charlie.

"He's adorable."

"Thank you," Sarah replied as the woman walked away.

With that, she pushed her cart to the checkout. It seemed so long since she really chatted with anybody. Though she felt certain she wouldn't be found, it always nagged as a possibility in the back of her mind.

"We do need to make some friends, Charlie," Sarah said as she snapped his car seat into the car. "I think it would be very good for us."

6

It was now early June and Sarah had accomplished a lot in the past few weeks. She was grateful that Charlie pretty much spent most of his time eating and sleeping. This allowed her to get her garden planted. The chicken wire fencing had proved to deter the rabbits. Her peas, lettuce, radishes, onions, and carrots were all growing nicely. They had a few soft rains, which were perfect for the garden. She was pleased with the soil, too. It seemed to be fertile enough, and because of its texture, she was confident that she would be harvesting nicely shaped veggies. The potato plants were just beginning to push through the ground. They also seemed to be thriving.

This week she had been leaving the seedlings outside on the porch at night to harden them off. Soon she would transplant them into the garden. She put the beans directly into the ground. Sarah couldn't help but to think of how wonderful it was going to be to have fresh beans! How wonderful all of this fresh food would be!

Today, she and Charlie made their weekly drive into town to fill up the water jugs. Sarah also brought a cooler for ice. She was getting to know the people at the small grocery store in Lone Pine and the owner let her take any of the broken ice bags for free. They were just a hindrance to him and he would throw them out anyways.

What happened during this trip to town took Sarah by surprise. While filling up her water jugs at Carson's Spring, the old man that she had seen the first time she stopped at the spring was waiting to get his fill of water. She only had two of the water bottles left to fill when she heard the commotion.

"Dag burn it!" the old man yelled.

Sarah looked over near his pickup truck to see several chickens running about. The man was locking up two of them in a wire cage that had apparently fallen from his truck. She saw one hen near the front of her car. Grabbing a large branch nearby, she walked slowly toward it. In one swift move, Sarah dropped the branch on top of the chicken, applying enough pressure to trap it among the branches and leaves. She crawled along the branch to her trapped prey. Quickly, she grabbed a leg and picked the hen up. It squawked and flapped until Sarah was able to gather it up and hold its wings down.

The man was walking toward her with two others in his arms. He also had a long rod with a dull hook at the end.

"Don't know how you caught 'er wit' out one of these," he said.

Sarah smiled. "I think it was all beginner's luck," she replied. "Are there any more?"

"Nope. That's it," he said as he locked the two chickens in the cage. Holding it closed with his hand, he turned to Sarah. "You can put 'er in here."

Sarah stepped around to the back of the pickup and slid the hen through the narrow slit he allowed. The back of his truck had four other crates filled with chickens, as well. They were all standing up straight with their heads turned to one side watching the ruckus.

"Name's Henry Jacobson. Folks just call me 'Hank,'" he said extending his hand.

"Sarah Brenny," she said, shaking his hand.

"Brenny, eh? You any relation to the Brennys on Lake Serene?"

Sarah looked at him for a moment. She didn't know how to answer. She didn't know anybody in her family, other than her mother. Sure, she knew her father, but he didn't matter in this situation. She didn't even know the name of the lake behind her cabin.

"My mother's name is Joan," she replied.

"Joan. And she has a sister named Liz and a brother named Bill. Oh yeah, I remember those three from the day they were born! I used to fish wit' yer great-gran' pappy out there on Lake Serene. You stayin' for the summer out there?"

"Yes, we are," Sarah said, thinking less was more at this point.

"Who's 'we'?"

"My son, Charlie, and me."

"Charlie?! Well, this I have got to see!" he said, walking over to her car.

Sarah followed closely behind him. Though she was certain the man meant no harm, her heart still pounded inside her chest. She knew very well that this man was not a *spy* for Larry. "You're just being paranoid," she thought to herself.

"Hi Charlie!" Hank lightly tapped a large knuckle on the window.

Sarah opened the door and unfastened Charlie from his car seat. The brightness of the day forced his eyes shut. Hank shielded them with his hand and Charlie opened his eyes again.

"So, you got saddled with yer great-great-grandpappy's name, eh? It's a good name. He was a good man," Hank spoke softly.

He turned to Sarah, "It's nice to meet a new generation."

Sarah smiled. "It's nice to meet you, too."

"I'd like to repay you fer yer help, but I'd only be able to pay you in chickens," he chuckled.

"What are you going to do with them?" Sarah asked.

"Oh, jus' thinnin' out the flock. Bringin' them to the auction barn. I won't get much for 'em, but its always fun to go there, anyway."

Sarah knew a little about chickens. They had them at the commune, for eggs and butchering.

"Are they laying hens?"

"Well, all hens are layin' hens, 'til they get old. Then they slow down. That's when they become stewin' hens. Heh-heh," responded Hank. "Did you want a couple fer the cabin?"

"I just thought it'd be nice…" started Sarah.

"You're welcome to 'em, but you'll need a place to lock 'em up at night or the critters will get 'em," he said.

"Yes, I suppose you're right. I don't think I'm ready for chickens." Her mind was busy thinking of where she could put them. There was that little shed in the clearing just south of the cabin, but it had no roof or door. She could perhaps fix it up, but that would really dip into her finances. Over time, she thought, she could scrape up what she needed to make that shed functional for next to free.

Hank watched Sarah think. "Why don't you follow me to the auction? You never know what people will bring in to get rid of," he suggested.

"How far away is it?" Sarah asked.

"Oh, 'bout five miles. Not far."

"It sounds interesting. I think we'll follow you out there. I've never been to an auction before."

"Well, alrighty! Let me fill up my jugs and we'll head out," Hank said with a happy smile.

7

It was easy for Sarah to follow Hank, being the Sunday driver that he was. Even so, it didn't take them long to get to the auction barn, and the roads this far north were pretty simple. It would be hard for her to get lost.

They parked their vehicles and Sarah arranged Charlie in his sling. She figured she had about an hour before he would need to be fed.

"You go in that door right there," Hank said, pointing. "And git yourself a number. Don't worry; they don't cost anything." It was as though he could

67

read her mind. "I have to bring in my chickens and I'll catch up wit' you."

Sarah went to get a number. The place was bustling with activity. Kids were running around, laughing and playing. Women congregated like hens in flocks of three or four, while the men seemed to be handling the business end of things. Everybody was having a great time.

It was Sarah's turn at the window to get her number.

"Driver's license, please," said the woman, pointing to a sign with her pen that read: "Please have your driver's license ready."

"Sorry," Sarah said, pulling her license out of her back pocket. (An essential item her mother had arranged for her.) The woman took Sarah's information and handed her a number.

"Thank you," said Sarah, returning her license to her pocket. As she made her way to the door, she saw Hank on the other side of the room.

"Go on and wait outside," he called over the crowd.

Sarah stepped outside away from the building. In one area she saw dozens of cages similar to the ones Hank had lined up. Chickens, geese, ducks, you name it. She walked along the row to see if she could recognize Hank's chickens. There were two cages that each contained a turkey.

Sarah stopped to look at them. They weren't particularly attractive up close.

She felt a tug at her elbow. "Look pretty tasty, don't they?" Hank asked, chuckling. And now that he mentioned it, Sarah had to agree. "Come 'ere. I wanna show you something."

She followed him through the crowd. The things that were to be auctioned off were all in rows with lot numbers assigned to them. A few rows away from the chickens, there were several lots of wood. Some were plank boards, some were posts. There were steel fence posts, too: much more heavy-duty than the ones Sarah had used around her garden.

Hank stopped. "You see? You never know what somebody wants to get rid of."

"How much does stuff like this usually go for?"

"Oh, it depends," Hank replied. "Being early June, it may go a little higher than it would, say in September, because people will have an immediate use for 'em. But I'd imagine this here roll of wire would probably go for twelve bucks," he said, kicking a used roll of woven wire. "It looks old, but you can see it still has life in it. It just all depends on who is here and what they're looking for."

Sarah couldn't help but think of the money she had spent to fence in her garden. "Water under the bridge," she thought.

"C'mon," Hank said. "They're starting over here."

Sarah again followed him.

The auctioneer had a microphone plugged in to a small speaker with a shoulder strap that he carried like a purse. Next to him was a man with a clipboard and a pen. At the first lot to be auctioned stood a boy of about 16 years, picking through the pile.

The auctioneer blew into his microphone. "Test. Test. Can you hear me in the back?"

"Yep!" came a call.

"Okay. Lot number one-eleven. We've got three five-gallon buckets, an anvil, a lawnmower, and baling twine."

The 16-year-old held the buckets and baling twine in the air.

"Thirty dollars! Who'll give me thirty?" the auctioneer called.

The crowd stood still.

"Come on, who'll give me thirty? The lawn mower works. After you cut your grass, you can bale it."

The crowd chuckled.

"Twenty-five, then. Who'll give me twenty-five?"

"Hep!" said the man with the clipboard.

"We've got twenty-five, who'll give me twenty-six?

"Hep!" said the man with the clipboard again, raising his hand in the direction that the bid came from.

"Twenty-six. Twenty-seven, twenty-seven…"

"Hep!"

"Twenty-eight, twenty-eight, who'll give me twenty-eight?"

"Hep!"

"Twenty-nine, twenty-nine…"

"Hep!"

"Thirty, thirty…"

"Hep!"

"Thirty-one, thirty-one, who'll give me thirty-one?"

Nobody bid.

"Sold for thirty dollars to…" the auctioneer looked at the man toward the back of the crowd holding his number up so it could be seen. "…to number fifty-four."

"Our next lot, lot number one-o-six, we have four stackable resin chairs, a charcoal grill, and a patio table with an umbrella. Everything you need to get the party started," the auctioneer continued.

"Wow," said Sarah to Hank, "they certainly don't waste time, do they?"

"Not on this stuff, they don't. The real auction is in the barn. It's a livestock auction," replied Hank.

"How often do they hold auctions?" Sarah asked.

Well, ones like this, usually every week, spring through fall. They sorta change with the seasons. Did you see anything you need?"

"I really didn't see too much, yet."

"'Cause there are a couple lots that if they were both bought, you could make a nice cage for chickens. Good enough to get you through a summer, anyway. C'mon, I'll show you," Hank said, walking away.

He walked a couple of rows away from where the auctioneer was and stopped in front of a pile of lumber. He kicked at it with his toe. "This here has all you'd need to frame up a cage and close in one end to keep 'em from the weather."

He walked on to another lot. "And this lot here has everything needed to wire it in."

Sarah looked the lots over, and while she thought that Hank probably knew what he was talking about, she was no carpenter.

"I'm not very handy with a hammer," she started to say.

"Now I'm glad you said that, Sarah, 'cause you see, I'd build the cage for you for a swap," Hank said.

"A swap?" Sarah was surprised. What could she possibly have that Hank would want?

"Yep. I'll build your cage if you let me fish Lake Serene. I ain't been there in years, an' if people obey "No Trespassing" signs, nobody else been there either."

Sarah looked at Hank. She didn't know what to say. She had to assume that Lake Serene was the lake her cabin was on, and that Hank really did know her family. Her mother did tell her to be friendly, and to fit right in. But was this being too impetuous?

"I'll even provide the chickens," Hank persisted.

"How about if we see what the lots go for, and we'll take it from there?" Sarah suggested.

"Alrighty. I can live by that," said Hank.

The auctioneer was one row away from the lumber and wire lots. She and Hank joined back with the crowd. Sarah was surprised at some of the things to be auctioned off. Actually a bit more disappointed than surprised because she had spent more money on the same items at stores and garage sales. "Water under the bridge," she reminded herself and thought what a large bridge it was getting to be!

"Our next lot, lot number twenty-nine, is for the ladies out there. We've got lots of canning jars. Pints, quarts, and jellies. A hot water bath canner, pressure cooker – still new in the box, and all sorts of lids, rims, and other miscellaneous stuff," the auctioneer said.

Sarah's ears perked up and she wiggled her way through the crowd to get a better look.

"Thirty dollars. Who'll give me thirty?"

The crowd remained still.

"Twenty-five, then. Who'll give me twenty-five?"

Still no bids.

Sarah decided not to be the opening bidder because she wanted to see how low the auctioneer would start even though she was willing to pay $25 for it.

"Come on, folks, this is good stuff. Ladies, you'll need it in a couple of months. The *Farmer's Almanac* predicts bumper crops this year," the auctioneer pleaded. "Twenty, twenty, who'll start me out at twenty?"

Still no bids.

"Fifteen, then. Fifteen. Who'll give me fifteen?"

"Hep!"

"That's more like it! Sixteen, sixteen…"

"Hep!"

"Seventeen, seventeen, who'll give me seventeen…"

"Hep!"

The bidding went on to what seemed like forever to Sarah. She had raised her number at $18, then $20. Her top dollar she'd go was 30. This, to her, was a very fair price to pay for all of those useful things. She needed that equipment to store her vegetables for the winter.

"Twenty-two, twenty-two, who'll give me twenty-two?"

Sarah raised her number.

"Hep!"

"Twenty-three, twenty-three, do I hear a twenty-three?"

The crowd was still again.

"Sold for twenty-two dollars to number two-seventeen," the auctioneer concluded, reading Sarah's bidding card.

Sarah turned around to tell Hank, but he was right beside her.

"You're a natural at this, Sarah! And you got a real good buy, if you can, that is. Heh-heh!"

Sarah felt as though she struck gold. This was a major necessity she could now cross off of her list. And for only $22! The brand new pressure canners that she had priced started at $70. And all of those jars and the canner, too! Sarah began to think about taking Hank up on his offer. "I'd have some fresh eggs," she thought, "and I could always butcher one if the need arises." Though the thought didn't please her. She wasn't sure if she could bring herself to butcher an animal. She did realize, however, that butchering was something that she would need to do, whether she liked it or not.

She looked at Hank. "Let's see if I can get those two lots you showed me as cheap as this lot I just bought."

Hank's eyes lit up, "You've got the bug, haven't you?" he laughed as they headed toward the lot with the lumber.

"I've looked the others over, and this lot here has the best wood for the job," Hank assured her.

"Okay," replied Sarah. "What is the most you would pay for it?"

Hank rubbed his chin, "Oh, I'd say its worth fifty or more, but I'd only pay about thirty. But I'm cheap."

"So am I, Hank. So am I," said Sarah.

Sarah walked out of the auction barn's office with her receipts, and Hank walked out with the money he made from selling his chickens.

Sarah was pleased. She paid only $19 for the wood, and only $8 for the wire.

"There is one problem, Hank," said Sarah.

"What's that?"

"I won't be able to get all that wood and wire in my car."

Hank looked at her. "Do you really think that's a problem, Sarah?"

"At least let me pay you for gas," she said.

"Nope. But what you can do is fry me up some of the fish I'm gonna catch on Lake Serene."

Sarah smiled, "It's a deal."

8

The sun was barely up the following day when Sarah heard Hank's truck coming down the driveway through the woods. He parked next to Sarah's car.

Sarah walked out with a cup of tea to greet him.

"Thank you, thank you," said Hank, taking the tea from her with both hands. He took a sip and looked around.

"Heh-heh! Place ain't changed a bit! Still no 'lectricity, eh? Surprised a gal yer age would put up without it. No television. No computer."

"I'm more of a book person, really," replied Sarah.

"Well, that just proves there's hope for the world yet," Hank chuckled and drank more tea.

"Come in and see the cabin," said Sarah.

"Nope, let me give you this cup back before I break it and unload my truck. Then I'll have a look around."

"I can help you. I just need to go get Charlie…" Sarah began.

"It won't take me long at all. You go deal with Charlie and I'll be done in two shakes," he said, already dropping the tailgate of his pickup.

Sarah went inside to get Charlie. She had fed him earlier and he fell back to sleep on the bed. She peeked at her sleeping baby and tucked at the little nest she had built around him with the bedding. By the time she returned outside, Hank was unloading the last of the wood and only had the rolls of wire left in his pickup.

Sarah walked over to the pile of building materials.

"I can build the cage right here. When I'm done, you'll be able to pull it around an' put it wherever you want it," Hank said. He kicked the last roll of wire off the tailgate and jumped off the end of the pickup truck the best a man of his age could. Sarah guessed he was about 70, but couldn't be certain.

It took Hank only about two hours to build the cage. Sarah worked in the garden transplanting tomatoes, squash, cucumbers, broccoli, and peppers. Though they were only about five to seven inches out of the ground, she staked the plants that she thought needed support.

Hank stepped over the chicken wire fence and looked around at the garden. "You plannin' on sellin' yer veg?" he asked.

Sarah stopped what she was doing and stood up. She took her gloves off and shook the dirt from them.

"No, Hank. Actually, I am planning on staying here for quite a while. It's all Charlie and I can afford at the moment."

Hank looked at her. Sarah couldn't tell what he was thinking. Finally he nodded and said, "Then you ought to raise rabbits, too."

Sarah smiled softly, relieved that he didn't come back with all sorts of reasons why she couldn't stay here. To her, she felt she had everything she needed, providing she would be able to can enough food to last her until the following year. Her largest concern still remained to be cutting enough wood. Which reminded her, she needed to cut her quota for the day. She allowed no slack in that area. She felt more confident about her wood pile everyday as it grew. She was now stacking it between the trees along the south side of the cabin. The weather had been warm enough where she didn't need to heat the cabin all night. The mornings could be a bit chilly, but the cabin warmed up quickly when she started a fire around five o'clock.

"How 'bout I catch us some fish for lunch?" Hank suggested, interrupting Sarah's thoughts.

"That sounds great!" Sarah said.

"I could use a hand getting the gear, though," Hank said, walking toward the cabin.

Sarah scurried after him. "I don't have any fishing gear, Hank."

Hank stopped and turned around. He looked puzzled for a moment, and then smiled. "You ain't seen the cellar, have you?"

Now the puzzled look was on Sarah's face.

"C'mon, I think you'll like this."

Sarah followed Hank into the cabin. She quickly peeked at Charlie.

Hank began to move the chairs from the table then moved the table itself. It was difficult to see in the faint light, but there was a door in floor of the cabin. With the cast iron handle used to lift the burners and to open the front of the fire box door of the wood stove, he pried the corner of the door up. Sliding his fingers underneath the door, he set the tool down then lifted the door with both hands. It was quite heavy, Sarah could tell. She felt the cold air fill the cabin. Hank let the door open until a rope attached to it tightened, allowing the door to lean back enough to stay open on its own. He reached inside the dark hole and pulled out an old railroad-styled lantern. He dusted it off with his hand and lit it, then hung it back on the peg from which he took it.

Sarah covered Charlie up with another quilt that was folded at the foot of the bed and walked slowly over to the hole in the cabin floor. The lantern lit up the small pit nicely and she was surprised to see what was inside.

"You'll need to climb down an' hand things up to me, Sarah," Hank said, cleaning cobwebs away with the broom. She approached the ladder slowly.

"Turn around and back down. It's easier."

She did as she was told. The ladder was made out of logs about three inches wide. She could tell it would be easy to slip on the round rungs. The cellar was only about six feet deep and the floor was just plain dirt. The walls were made of stone and had shelves running the length of them. There was an old wooden rocking chair covered with dust and cobwebs.

"Hand me that chair first, so we can git 'er out of the way," instructed Hank. Sarah picked it up by the arms and held it as high as she could. Hank grabbed the back of it and pulled it up. Sarah pushed on the rockers to help, for it was quite heavy. She heard it thud on the floor above her when Hank set it down. He got back on his knees and peered into the cellar. "Hand up those oars next, then the poles and tackle box," he said, pointing.

As Sarah did so, she asked, "Is there a boat somewhere?"

"A canoe and a paddle boat, if no one stole 'em."

"I didn't see them anywhere," said Sarah.

"Probably 'cause you don't know where to look," said Hank, chuckling. "You may as well grab that gun and ammo, too. And anything else you might want."

Sarah found the gun and a few boxes of shells. She handed it all up to Hank. She looked around the space. "What's this, Hank?" she asked, holding a bundle of iron rods.

"That's a tripod."

Sarah looked at him blankly.

"For cookin' outside. You'll probably want it for the summer."

She handed the bundle up to him. She looked along the shelves of the cellar. A few canned goods, a large trash bag that felt to contain a quilt or blanket, some candles, cast iron pans, and a few empty baskets. On one wall there was an old trunk that was kept up off the dirt floor with a couple of logs underneath it. "What's in the trunk?" she asked, both nervous to open it and eager to get out of the cold hole.

"Oh, that's just all personal family stuff. You'll probably like to go through that some time," Hank replied.

"I think I will, but not now. It's cold down here. I think I've got all I want for now," she said, stepping up on to the ladder.

As she began to climb, she noticed something behind the ladder. She stepped back down; this time she carried the lantern with her. A big smile spread across her face. "A chainsaw!" she exclaimed.

9

While Hank went down to Lake Serene to fish, Sarah took the rocking chair outside and dusted it off. It was a good-sized chair with a high back, large seat, and wide arm rests. She could tell by the way the wood was worn smooth, that in the past this chair had been somebody's favorite. She left it outside on the porch and went into the cabin to get Charlie. His eyes tightened as she brought him out into the daylight. Though the porch had a roof, it was still quite a bit brighter than inside the cabin.

"Look what Mommy found, Charlie! I think you'll like this!" She sat down in the rocker and rocked with Charlie cradled in her arms. Sarah found the rocker to be very comfortable, and how nice it was to have arm rests! She let herself lean back and relax as she rocked gently while Charlie nursed. She stared ahead at her garden and was pleased at how well it was coming along. She looked at the cage that Hank had built for her chickens. It was about six feet wide by eight feet long and only perhaps two feet tall. One end was enclosed so the chickens would be able to get out of the weather. That was also where they would go to lay their eggs, Hank had explained. He put the top on with hinges so Sarah could easily open it and gather the eggs each day. She thought of the luxury of having fresh eggs each morning.

Sarah awoke with a jerk and her arms tightened around Charlie. She had nodded off in her new favorite chair! She heard whistling coming up from the lake and she could hear the light jingle of the metal fish stringer. "He must have caught enough for lunch," she thought.

Hank propped his pole up against the porch rail and set the tackle box down. He held up the stringer. "Look 'ere!" he exclaimed. "I think they all just grew bigger and fatter these past few years waitin' for me to come back!"

There were four large sunfish and a good-sized bass on the stringer.

"I was lucky with the bass. I usually only catch them in the morning." Hank had such a smile on his face, Sarah couldn't help but giggle. "You've got the best fishin' spot for all around, Sarah, and my advice is you keep it to yerself. Once you let one person in, they'll all be here poundin' on yer door. 'Course I already have permission," he smiled.

"They look just wonderful, Hank! I trust the canoe was still down there," said Sarah.

"Yep. And the paddleboat."

Hank carried the fish over to his truck and dropped the tailgate. He put a piece of board that had been left over from the chicken pen on the tailgate and set the fish beside it. He walked back toward the cabin and took a fillet knife out of the tackle box.

"You ever fillet a fish, Sarah?" he asked.

Sarah shook her head.

"Well, come and watch. You'll learn somethin' good," Hank said.

Sarah went into the cabin and grabbed the sling. She nestled Charlie into it and walked over to Hank's truck.

He showed her with each fish how to fillet it. She thought she'd be able to remember how to do it when the need arose, though she was not looking forward to it.

"Most important is you'll want to get rid of all of this," Hank said, pointing to the pile of heads and guts with the fillet knife. "You can bring it away from the cabin for the critters to eat, or what I suggest is that you either burn 'em or throw 'em back in the lake. Then the critters will have nothin' to come after. And you'll want to always wash everything up real good. Fish stink and the smell itself will attract a lot of unwanted visitors."

Hank looked up at the porch and saw a garden spade. He took the spade and dug out a small pit near the edge of the hill that overlooked Lake Serene. Next he gathered several good-sized rocks that were beside the cabin and arranged them around the pit. In the pit, he started a little fire and fed it more and more wood until it was burning good and hot. He took the fish parts to the fire and threw them on, a few pieces at a time.

"Suppose I should have a bucket of water right here. Just in case. You got a bucket, Sarah?"

"Yes, but I could just bring you a jug of water," Sarah said.

"Nope. That's alright. I'll just fill the bucket."

He took the bucket and walked over to the woods south of the cabin. Sarah watched him. He walked along the tire path into the woods. She thought he must have been heading to the river for water and wondered why he didn't just go to the lake for it. It was closer, after all.

He turned off of the path and went into the trees. The leaves were full now and she could no longer see him. She turned back to check on the fire. She could smell the fish parts as they burned but could also tell the smell would quickly go away.

Hank came back out of the woods without the bucket.

"What happened?" Sara asked.

"Pump needs primin'," replied Hank. "I'll need a jug of water after all."

"Pump?"

"Yeah. You've got a pump 'ere, Sarah. Yer ancestors didn't live in the dark ages. Heh-heh. But she needs primin' and I'll oil 'er up a bit."

Sarah handed Hank a jug of water after he had retrieved a toolbox from his truck. She was pleased as punch to know that there was a well on the property. She watched the fire as it burned down to mere coals and threw a couple shovelfuls of dirt on top of it to smother it out. She and Charlie walked down the tire path, looking into the woods for Hank. It didn't take long to spot him. He was pumping the long handle of the pump. Nothing was coming out.

"Did it go dry?" Sarah asked, approaching him.

"Nope. I doubt that. It's just that it hasn't been used for so long. The water needs to be coaxed back up the pipe. It'll come."

"Is this water drinkable?"

Hank looked up at her. "Sure is. This is a nice deep well. You probably will forget all about Carson's."

Sarah watched as he continued to pump, thinking that this modern convenience was going to be so useful. She began to think how fortunate it was for her to have met Hank. Who knew how long it would have been before she discovered the root cellar, the boats, or the pump. Though she hesitated, she asked him, "Hank, could you show me how to work that chainsaw?"

"Sure can! It might need some work, though." He replied. "I can hear the water gurgling. It won't be long now…" His words were interrupted by some brownish water coming out of the spout.

Sarah frowned at the sight. Hank laughed.

"Heh-heh! Don't be concerned. It'll clear up real quick." He continued pumping and the water lightened as it came out faster and faster. Soon it was just as clear as the water from Carson's Spring. "Cup yer hands and have a taste."

Sarah cupped her hands together and let the water run over them. It was very cold. She took a drink.

"That's water, alright," she said, wiping her mouth on her shirt.

"Heh-heh," chuckled Hank as he hung the bucket on the spout and filled it up. Sarah filled the jug up, too.

"Now, so long as you use this frequently, you should be fine. Not much can go wrong on it," he said.

"What about in the wintertime? Will it freeze up?"

"It can. But if you pump 'er slow at the end so the water just trickles out, you're likely to avoid that problem. You really ought to have a pump house around it, too," Hank said. He grabbed the bucket and the jug. "Now let's go eat those fish before something else does."

Sarah fried up a portion of the fish along with some potatoes and onion. She poured two cups of the water they had brought back from the pump. Hank raised his cup and said, "Here's to deep wells."

Sarah clanked her cup against his and replied, "Here is to good people like you."

Hank looked at Sarah. He wasn't expecting that. He actually blushed. "Thank you kindly, Sarah," he said softly, clanking her cup again.

"Well, Hank, it's true. I've known you barely twenty-four hours and you have made such a difference in Charlie and my life. Not only have you made it easier, you've made it more enjoyable."

The cabin was quiet and still. Sarah felt perhaps she made Hank a bit uncomfortable. To lighten the mood, she quickly added, "Now, tell me all about my family. I'd love to hear your stories."

Hank talked on and on, reminiscing of the old days. How he would hunt and fish these parts with her great-grandfather and her grandfather. How her great-grandfather was born and raised in this log cabin.

"There used to be a barn, too," Hank was saying as he helped Sarah wash the dishes.

"Yes," she said, "I saw that over in the next clearing. The roof is gone, though." She dried the last plate and set it on the shelf.

"Nope. That was just a shed. The barn was about four times as big as this cabin an' it had a loft, too. Burnt to the ground. Terrible time, that was. Yer great-gran'pappy lost near all his cows and one of his horses. All the hay fer the winter, too."

"Oh, how awful," said Sarah, picking Charlie up from the bed. She changed him and sat down with him in the rocker near the stove. Hank sat by the table and continued to tell her stories of her mother and her siblings on their summer vacations. Sarah was sure that her mother must have missed her family terribly. From what Hank had to say, they seemed very close.

"You think she'll come to visit anytime soon? I'd like to see her again."

Sarah thought quickly of how she could answer the question without needing to explain her situation and, at the same time, without telling a lie.

"I am hoping so, Hank. When she does, I'll be sure to let you know," was Sarah's reply.

It wasn't Hank's nature to pry, and Sarah appreciated that. He simply said, "You do that."

Sarah lifted Charlie up to her shoulder and patted his back gently until he let out a soft burp.

"Well, I best be gittin' on. Got a few chores of my own to tend to. I'll bring by the chickens in the next day or so," said Hank.

Sarah stood up and walked him out to the porch. "Thank you, again, Hank. For everything."

"Glad to do it. It's nice being back here again. I've always liked this place," replied Hank. "See you soon." He waved his hand over his head as he walked toward his truck.

10

Sarah changed the water in the galvanized tank that was designed specifically for watering chickens. Hank had given it to her when he brought the chickens over: five hens and one rooster. She felt bad that they were confined to the cage, but it was for their own safety. Hank had told her to leave them in the cage for about three weeks, then to prop one corner of the cage up so they could get out underneath it, but also could get back in to their water and feed. He had also brought a large gunny sack full of chicken feed, which they had transferred into the large storage bin that had been sitting at the foot of the bed. She put the bin on the porch next to the kindling. "One more week, my little chickadees, and you'll be able to explore a bit more," she said as she lowered the shallow pan of feed into the pen. She sprinkled some on the ground within the cage for them to scratch and peck at, as well.

The chickens clucked and pecked at their food. They seemed quite content in their new home. Sarah knew that one of them must be content because she found an egg! Hank told her it would take a while for them to feel comfortable enough to lay, but assured her that they would, eventually.

Sarah was excited about her first egg. She picked it up out of its nest and looked at it. It was brown and larger than the eggs she had purchased at the store. She looked at the five other nests. All of them had obviously been sat in, as the straw was shaped and contained a few feathers. All of them, however, were empty. She wondered which of her hens had laid the egg.

Her thoughts were interrupted when she heard Hank's truck. She could always hear it before she could see it. She closed the lid over the nesting boxes and cupped the egg in her hand. Hank couldn't help but notice the wide grin on her face as she walked toward him.

"It's a bit early to be up to somethin', ain't it?" he asked.

Sarah raised her arm, holding the egg between her thumb and first two fingers.

"Heh-heh! So, the red hen laid first, eh?"

Sarah looked at him in surprise. "How do you know that?!"

"Size of the egg. An' the color," replied Hank. "All of 'em will be brown, but probably not that dark, and the red hen lays the largest eggs. If you want more chickens, she's the one I'd let set."

"Should I put it back?"

"Naw. You enjoy it. She'll lay another one tomorrow. But if you want to hurry her settin' along, an' if the other hen's git to layin', you can add their eggs to the red hen's clutch and she'll start settin' sooner. A hen will only set on as many eggs as she can keep warm. No more."

"How long does it take for them to hatch?"

"Twenty-one days or so," said Hank, walking toward the cabin. "Yer garden is looking real good, Sarah."

"Yes, I have to agree! I've been enjoying the radishes and lettuce so far. Another month and I'll have very little reason to go to town."

"Just for yer dry goods and church," said Hank.

Sarah picked Charlie up off the bed. He was growing quickly. "Hank, do you know of a good doctor for Charlie?" she asked as she changed the baby.

"Well, there's Dr. Greene. He's the young, new-fangled one. Then there's Doc James, he's been here fer forty years or so now. Took over his daddy's practice. He's the one I'd pick. He won't give you a pill every time yer nose runs, though. If that's what you want, you best go to Doc Greene.

"I think I'm more interested in Dr. James," said Sarah. "Sit in the rocker and you can hold Charlie while I make us some tea."

Hank sat down and cradled Charlie while rocking him gently. "Open the gate an' let me in... toll first you pay...I have no gold, what shall I do? Turn and go away," he sang to Charlie.

Sarah went outside to get the hot water for their tea. She had set up a little cooking station about twenty feet from the cabin. The tripod was set up on one side, where she hung her Dutch oven over the fire. On the other side was a small pit where she could balance her enamelware coffee pot over a small fire on a circle of rocks. Some days were just too warm for a fire in the wood stove. The thick log walls were very effective at insulating the cabin. Hank told her they would help keep the cabin cooler in the summer and yet help keep it warm in the winter.

She smiled as she listened to Hank sing his songs to Charlie. She made two cups of tea, using the wood stove as a countertop, and then returned the pot to the fire outside. Hank stood up from the rocker and handed Charlie to Sarah.

"I got that old chainsaw workin'. But I can't guarantee how long she'll last," Hank said.

"Even if it's a day, I'll be ahead," replied Sarah.

"I thought I'd cut a bunch of wood for you today in exchange for some fishin'."

Sarah smiled, "Of course! I couldn't refuse an offer like that!" She knew that Hank knew he didn't have to do these odd jobs just to fish on Lake Serene. It was just his way of helping out. Hank truly enjoyed being at the cabin. He was one of the longtime residents of Lone Pine and many of his friends had either passed away or had been moved into nursing homes. Sarah felt that he got lonely, and sometimes just wanted to spend the day here at Lake Serene, so he'd come up with excuses to drop by. She was glad he did, too. She felt his company was good for her and Charlie.

"I must say, though, that I'm proud of myself with how much wood I have cut by hand! I have a few nice stacks between the trees out there," said Sarah.

"I'm inclined to agree with you on that point." Hank set his cup down on the table. "On that note, I'm gonna git started."

Sarah knew better than to offer to help. She knew that he would go fishing afterwards and she'd fry up his catch for him.

Sarah heard Hank's truck rumbling toward the cabin. He had driven down the driveway and parked somewhere out near the road to cut the wood. Throughout the morning she heard him working with the chainsaw. Now he was backing the pickup to the large stump that Sarah used for splitting. He dropped the tailgate and started to throw the round logs onto the ground. Charlie was sleeping, so Sarah came out to help. She was impressed at how much wood there was!

"Oh, Hank! I cannot thank you enough!" she exclaimed.

"Maybe you best wait until after you split and stack it all," Hank chuckled. "You got a lot of fallen trees around here that are plenty good for firewood. Already nice and dry. Should make for some easier splitting."

Sarah could care less about all the work she faced splitting the wood. Just the fact that she didn't need to cut it first with her pruning saw, which was becoming quite dull, was a great relief to her.

"You'll have to show me how to work that chainsaw, Hank," she said.

"I'll show you, but you ought not use it unless another body is around. I've heard of many accidents and lives lost because of these things. People traipsing off alone to cut wood, then cut themselves an' wind up bleedin' to death," Hank advised.

Sarah nodded. "You've cut twice as much wood this morning than I have in the past month!" she said, feeling a large burden lifted from her shoulders.

"Yep, an' I say I keep cuttin'. If I come out a couple times a week for a bit, you'll have more wood than you'll know what to do with. It looks like yer gonna have a bumper crop of apples, too."

"Apples? Where is there an apple tree?"

"Out by the road. There are five or six trees."

"Well, I'll have to be certain to can some for pies and make applesauce," said Sarah.

"I love apple pie," Hank said, kicking a large stump off of the tailgate.

11

Over the next couple of weeks, Hank came out to cut wood for Sarah. He was methodically working his way through the woods starting near the road and then heading toward the cabin. Each day Sarah would split as much wood as time allowed. Her woodpile was growing quickly. Alongside the cabin, she had stacked piles between the trees about five feet high. Hank was right; it did look as though she were fencing herself in.

Sarah stood on the end of the porch and smiled. She was confident that she had enough wood to last her all winter and right into spring. She drank the last of her tea and picked up the basket of laundry to be done. At one of the auctions, she had found a large copper boiler and washboard. These made laundry day much more bearable, though it was about her least favorite chore. It was hard on the hands and seemed to take forever.

While she was hanging the last few diapers on the line, she heard Hank's truck approaching. She wondered why he came today, since he was just here yesterday. Hank got out of the truck. He was in clean, neat clothes. His face was freshly shaven and his hair had been combed back.

"What's up?" Sarah asked.

"It's Fourth of July. I thought you and Charlie would want to come to town with me for the festivities. It's a lot of fun!"

Sarah thought of all the work she had planned to do today. For some reason, she always seemed to get more done when Hank wasn't there, probably because they always stopped to have lunch and wound up chatting for an hour. She didn't mind, though. She knew it was good for her to relax like that every so often.

Looking at Hank all dressed up, she didn't have the heart to tell him no. "We'd love to, if you can give us time to get ready!" Sarah said with a big smile.

"You bet," said Hank. "You go on in an' get ready. I'll take care of things out here."

Sarah brought Charlie into the cabin and looked through his clothes. She found a small pair of blue denim shorts and a white T-shirt that had red trim on it. "Perfect!" she thought. She put on clean clothes herself and brushed her hair, still putting it in a ponytail. After gathering up a few necessities, she put them into her backpack.

Meanwhile, Hank had put the fire out, rounded the chickens up, and let the cage down. He brought the empty laundry basket up to the porch. Poking his head inside the door, he asked, "You ready?"

Sarah stood up and said, "Yep! Why don't we take my car since the car seat is already strapped in?"

"Makes no difference to me," said Hank.

Sarah secured Charlie into the carrier and picked up the backpack.

"If you'll just grab that stroller, Hank, we can be on our way."

Hank grabbed the stroller and the backpack from Sarah's hand. Sarah locked the cabin up, double-checking that the door was secure. She opened the trunk of her car for Hank and snapped

Charlie's carrier into its base in the back seat. He was just dozing off, content with a belly full of milk.

Lone Pine was as busy as Sarah had ever seen it. The majority of the festival was set up in the large parking lot at the church. They had to park nearly a mile away, and then walk back to the festival. Sarah was glad she had brought her stroller, though she wasn't certain how long Charlie would tolerate it. He wasn't sitting up on his own yet, but could hold his head up just fine.

As they got closer to the church, Sarah could see the people lined up on either side of the street. Kids were sitting on the ground while parents stood behind them. Hank tugged at Sarah's arm. "Let's park it right here," he said. "The parade will come right by us."

They fell into formation at the end of the line of people. Charlie looked around at all the waving flags and laughing children. Sarah turned his stroller so the awning kept him in the shade. Soon she could hear the band coming closer and then saw the first parade float slowly making its way toward them.

It wasn't all that fancy, just a hay wagon with lots of red, white, and blue crepe paper. There were some kids, perhaps eight to ten years old, tossing candy into the crowd while Uncle Sam sat in a chair in the center, waving to the crowd. Two draft horses pulled the hay wagon with a young man driving them. He waved to Hank and tipped his straw hat at Sarah.

"That's my grandson!" Hank exclaimed, waving back.

Sarah smiled and waved. She hadn't met any of Hank's family yet, but she felt like she knew them after hearing Hank talk about them. She'd like to meet his family.

Next came a marching band. The horns were loud. Sarah looked at Charlie to see if he was scared. He had a concerned look on his face, but he wasn't crying. She squatted next to him and patted his leg.

Following the band were a bunch of kooky clowns running around and teasing the children lined up along the street. One clown ran right toward Sarah and Charlie with a wooden bucket. Sarah prepared herself to get soaked with water and put her body in front of Charlie. The clown threw the water from the bucket onto Sarah's back. Only it wasn't water, it was just confetti and candy.

She laughed and looked at Hank with mild embarrassment. Several of the nearby children scrambled to grab the candy that was on the ground then quickly went back to their positions in front of their parents.

The end of the parade was followed up by some of the older children who just tagged along behind, throwing candy that they had gathered earlier back into the crowd. It was a short parade. At least that was Sarah's impression. She had never been to a parade before, but had seen glimpses of them on television. Those parades were extravagant with thousands of people crowding to watch. There were only about 200 people in this Lone Pine crowd and they were all heading back toward St. Joseph's for fun and games.

"C'mon over here," Hank said. He was walking the opposite way of the crowd. Sarah followed, pushing the stroller.

"Where are we going?"

"To go talk with Henry."

"Your grandson?"

"Yep! Nice name, eh?" Hank chuckled.

They were walking back in the direction they had parked her car, but then took a side street about three blocks in. On one side of the street were houses, but across from the houses it was all open field. In the field there were a couple of tractors, a bus that was being loaded with the marching band instruments, and Hank's grandson with his horses. He was taking the harnesses off of them while they

110

drank from a large rubber tub filled with water, and then began to brush their coats. The closer they got to the horses, the slower Sarah walked. They were enormous. Even though she was more than ten feet away, she felt as though she could be kicked at any moment.

"Come over this way, they won't get you," Hank said to Sarah.

She followed his instructions and now was near the back of the trailer, watching the two giants chomp on their hay. They looked at Sarah and Charlie from where they were tied to the side of the trailer, then turned back to focus on the hay Henry had put out for them.

"Henry, this 'ere is Sarah. The girl I told you about on Lake Serene."

Henry extended his hand, but Sarah hadn't noticed. He had the bluest eyes she had ever seen.

"Sorry, about that," Henry said as he brushed his hand on his jeans then extended it again.

"Oh, no, I'm sorry," Sarah said and put her hand out for him to shake.

Henry's hand was strong and warm. Sarah felt her cheeks flush and hoped that her face wasn't turning red.

"Grandpa has told us a lot about you. He's not being a nuisance, is he?" Henry laughed as he poked Hank in the ribs with an elbow.

111

"Oh, not at all!" said Sarah, trying not to stare at Henry's pleasant face. "We look forward to his visits. He has been so helpful to us."

"That's good to hear," said Henry as he squatted in front of the stroller. "And you must be Charlie. I've heard a lot about you, too!"

Charlie looked at Henry and kicked his feet a bit. Henry gently shook his hand, which looked tiny in comparison.

"You guys headed to the church?" Henry asked as he stood up.

"Yep. I gotta get my name in for the meat raffle," said Hank.

"Well, if you wait a few minutes, I'll walk with you."

Henry locked up the trailer and his truck. He checked the leads that tied his horses to the trailer and dumped a five-gallon bucket of water into the rubber tub.

"Okay, let's go!"

They took a back street toward the church. Sarah could see the steeple and hear the excitement that was going on. Every now and then a firecracker or bottle rocket would go off. She pushed the stroller while Hank and Henry walked just ahead of her. While they chatted away, Sarah thought about how handsome Henry was and hoped he didn't sense that she thought that about him. He was tall and had a strong build. And that smile!

Henry turned around. "You guys still with us?"

"Yes," Sarah said quietly. It was all she could get out. "What is the matter with you, Sarah?!" she thought to herself. "Pull yourself together."

"Okay then," replied Henry. He turned around and resumed talking with his grandpa. Sarah was upset at herself for being so tongue-tied. She felt like a schoolgirl experiencing her first crush.

"Think of something to say. Something *normal*," she thought. They were just approaching the church when it came to her.

"Henry, what are…" she started.

"Hen-ry! Over here!" a girl called from one of the booths. Henry looked in the girl's direction. "Come win a prize from me, Henry!" she called.

"Maybe later," Henry answered, smiling and waving.

"You better!" she called back, giving Henry an exaggerated pouty look.

Sarah looked at the girl. She was pretty with long blonde hair and bouncy curls at the ends. She sighed and forgot all about the conversational question she had concocted.

"The meat raffle booth is here, Grandpa," Henry said. He turned to Sarah, "Are you going to enter, too? It's only one dollar per ticket."

"Oh, I don't think so. Charlie doesn't eat much, yet."

"No, I suppose he doesn't!" Henry laughed. "Well, I'll buy five just to improve your odds, Grandpa."

"Okay, Henry, you do that," said Hank.

Sarah waited and watched as the two of them filled out their tickets and dropped them into a large box with a small slit cut into the top.

"Okay! My work here is done," said Hank, rubbing his hands together. "What should we do first?"

"Let's go to the shooting gallery and see how we do," suggested Henry. "Sound good to you, Sarah?"

"Sure," said Sarah. She tried to throw some enthusiasm into her response.

While Henry and Hank shot at the targets, Sarah's mind kept drifting back to that girl at the booth. She tried to get her brain to think rationally. She had just met Henry. It was not as though they were a couple. For all she knew, he could have a girlfriend. For all she knew, his girlfriend could be the girl at the booth! "Besides, I'm in no position to even be considering dating. And what makes me

115

think Henry would even be attracted to me?" Her thoughts continued to ramble until Charlie started to fuss.

"I think I better change him," she said. "We'll be right back."

"We'll be right 'ere," said Hank, aiming at a duck with a target in the middle of it.

Sarah pushed the stroller toward the entry that led into the church basement. She remembered seeing the restrooms sign at the rummage sale. Tipping the stroller back, she rolled Charlie down the steps on the back wheels. The basement smelled of food. Women in aprons and hairnets scurried around in a kitchen that Sarah didn't realize was there until now. Other than the kitchen and restrooms, the basement was one large space. In the center of the space, some tables were set up for people to eat at, mostly elderly people or mothers with small children. The walls of the basement were lined with tables where women were selling their handcrafts.

Sarah pushed the stroller through the restroom door and was relieved to see a changing station mounted to the wall. She changed Charlie quickly. He was still awake and alert. Sarah decided to nurse him for a few moments since there was a short couch in the powder area of the restroom. Charlie ate eagerly at first, but soon slowed down and fell asleep. Sarah gently strapped him back into the stroller and pushed it back to Hank and Henry.

They were in the same position as when she had left, laughing and having a good time.

"Did you win anything?" she asked.

"Not yet," they answered in unison.

They finished up the round they were on and called it quits. Henry turned to Sarah. "You wouldn't think we were hunters, would you?"

Sarah smiled. "The sights must be off."

"That's exactly what we think!" he laughed. He looked down at Charlie. "Well, he tuckered out on us."

Hank looked, too. "Yep. I've noticed that about him. Bright-eyed one minute, sound asleep the next."

"What would you like to do, Sarah?" Henry asked, sweeping his hand in front of him at all of the different booths.

"Oh, I don't know. I'm not familiar with any of these games," she said.

"Well, let's walk around. If one intrigues you, we'll stop and play."

"Alright," she replied, fighting off that silly schoolgirl feeling.

They walked around the large lot, playing an occasional game. Sarah hated to spend any money; but she did wind up spending $5 because she was too embarrassed to let Henry know that she had no income. True to his nature, Hank stood by quietly, letting Sarah maintain her pride. And although nobody won any prizes, they all had fun.

"Let's head over to the rides," Henry suggested.

"I'm not getting on any of those rickety things," Hank countered.

"You can watch Charlie while Sarah and I ride."

Sarah looked at Henry, then at Hank. "I'll take good care of him, Sarah. Besides, you'll be able to see us from the ride, for the most part."

"Alright, we'll see," she said.

The group walked a couple of blocks from the church where there were a dozen or so rides set up among more food and game booths. Sarah looked around at the rides and began to lean towards Hank's sentiment about them. As though sensing this, Henry said, "How about the Ferris wheel? It's not very big, goes slow, and you'll be able to see Grandpa and Charlie from it."

"Okay," said Sarah.

"Great! I'll go get the tickets!" Henry ran off before Sarah could change her mind. Within a minute, he was back and not even winded, Sarah noticed. Of course she did, she seemed to notice everything about him.

"C'mon," Henry gently grabbed Sarah's wrist and pulled her toward the line to get on the ride. Sarah went along with him but kept looking back at Charlie. It almost felt as though her body was going forward but her feet were going backward. Hank shooed her with his hand. She knew he would keep a close eye on Charlie, but somehow that didn't seem to make this separation easier.

Henry handed the boy at the gate two tickets and he let them pass. They sat in the next available seat and a man locked the safety bar in front of them. The ride slowly shifted forward, then stopped, and the next couple got in their seat. The ride shifted again and again until all of the seats were full. The music started and the wheel went slowly around. Henry would look at the countryside around them, pointing things out to Sarah. But her eyes seemed glued to Charlie. Her hands were wrapped tightly around the bar in front of her. Henry put his large hand over hers, "Sarah, relax. He is okay. Enjoy the sights. You don't see this view everyday. Look! There's Suzie and Elaine!"

Sarah looked in the direction he was pointing. That whole feeling of what she could only describe as unjustified jealousy came over her. Then she had to laugh. He was pointing at his truck and trailer. She could see the two horses.

"What's so funny?"

"Oh, nothing really. I was just going to ask you what your horses' names were earlier, and then I forgot to."

"Oh," said Henry. His eyebrows lifted, then dropped, not really understanding the humor. "Do you see that silo with the black and white checkered trim? That's Grandpa's place."

Sarah began to relax and enjoy the sites. Even though she didn't realize it, she was looking at Charlie and Hank every ten seconds.

"Can you see my place from here?"

Henry grinned. "You can't see your cabin, but do you see that huge clump of trees that is pretty much surrounded by fields? That's it, right there."

Sarah looked then waited until their seat came around to the top and looked again. It looked like an island.

"So many people have made offers on that place, but your family never wants to sell."

"I don't blame them," said Sarah, who had come to love her humble little home. Sure, it was a lot of work, but she felt so free there.

"Nor do I," replied Henry.

The ride stopped with a jerk. Sarah looked down. The man was unloading the seats. She was sort of sad it ended, but was glad to be back on the ground with Charlie.

"See anything you liked?" Hank asked her with a twinkle in his eye.

"It was beautiful," said Sarah. She had a large grin on her face.

"Anybody hungry?" Henry asked, looking at his watch. "It's almost one-thirty."

Before Sarah could answer, Hank said, "Yep! And I'm buying. Let's go get some hotdogs and root beer."

"You're on! I have to hustle, though. I'm scheduled to give hayrides at two-thirty. How'd you like to go for a hay ride?" Henry asked, looking at Sarah.

She was caught off guard. "Oh, I'd love to, but really, I better get home so Charlie can take a decent nap. I think he's had enough of the stroller. You don't mind, do you, Hank?"

"Not at all. I can stop back if I want. The fair is on 'til Sunday, anyway. You workin' everyday, Henry?"

"No, just today and tomorrow for hayrides, and a bit on Monday for cleanup."

Sarah ate her hotdog and listened while Henry and Hank continued to talk about the fair, the weather, and farm crops. She was impressed with the genuine kindness Henry seemed to have.

"He is just so *nice*," she thought. "And handsome! Don't forget about how handsome he is!" part of her mind seemed to be shouting, while another part was saying, "Calm down. Yes, he's handsome. What does that matter to you?"

"Sarah?"

Sarah snapped out of her daydream and looked up at Hank and Henry. For a second, she wondered if they had heard what was going on in her brain.

"Are you about ready to leave?" Hank asked again.

"Yes. Yes, I am."

"Are you okay?"

"Yes. I'm just a bit tired, is all. It must have been all the excitement."

"It was a pleasure to meet you, Sarah," said Henry, extending his had to her once again.

She put her hand in his. "The pleasure was mine, Henry. You must come by with your grandpa sometime."

Henry grinned, "Be careful what you wish for!" He picked up his straw hat, combed his fingers back through his sandy hair and put the hat on his head. "See you later, Grandpa!"

Sarah watched Henry as he walked away. And Hank watched Sarah, smiling to himself as he finished his root beer.

12

It was a beautiful day in early August. Sarah and Charlie were out for a walk in the woods. She now had this system down pat: Charlie in his sling, a backpack on her back, her trusty walking stick, and a large hunting knife in its sheath strapped around her hip.

In her backpack, she carried water, an apple, matches, zip lock bags, and a fresh snippet of wormwood. Wormwood was a plant that had been a standard at the cabin since it was built. Hank said her family used it to ward off insects, and Sarah had no reason to doubt this. On their many walks, Sarah would fill her baggies with the berries she would come across. Her favorite were the strawberries, though they were small. She thought she might buy a few plants next spring and start a patch near the cabin.

Whenever they ventured out into a new area of the woods, Sarah took the time to tie a bit of bed sheet to branches along the way. She had torn a bright pink sheet into strips about two inches wide and 12 inches long. Each strip had a number written on it in permanent marker. When it was time to head back to the cabin, the bright tags were easy to spot, and the numbers let her know she was directly on her path.

She felt small among the tall trees and the thought of being lost out in the woods overnight was not appealing to her. There were bears and coyotes living there, and while she had grown used to hearing them at night, she had no interest in meeting them.

During today's expedition, she made a terrific discovery. As she was sitting on a fallen tree to rest, about 75 feet away from her stood a plum tree full of fruit! She scanned the area and spotted six more. Taking a big swig of her water, she capped the bottle and returned it to her backpack. She pulled out three gallon-sized zip lock bags and began to fill them with plums, taking care not to pack them so tightly that they would bruise. She couldn't help but to eat a couple of them right then and there.

"Oh, Charlie! These are going to make some delicious canned plums for the wintertime!" she said. "We are going to have to come back for more."

She placed the bags carefully in her backpack and started walking back to the cabin. Normally, she would gather all of her pink markers. However, this time she left them tied where they were so she could easily locate the plum trees again.

Although she had walked for over an hour on her way into the woods, it took her only half that time to walk back out. As she approached the clearing where the cabin was, she had to stop and look at her home. The small cabin looked so friendly and inviting with the rocking chair on the porch and the colorful chickens scratching and pecking in the grass.

Her garden was beginning to burst with produce. For several weeks now, Sarah had been enjoying leaf lettuce salads with radishes, peas, green onions, cucumbers, and, occasionally, a tomato on top. She would make a simple dressing out of vinegar and oil. Sometimes she would crush raspberries and whisk them into the dressing.

This afternoon she would attempt to make some dill and some bread 'n' butter pickles while Charlie napped. She knew she was in for a busy fall with all of the canning that had to be done. She intended to can enough food to last her until next summer when the garden would be producing again. She still had money, should she need to buy food, but her goal was to spend that only on things like flour, sugar, salt, and other basics and necessities. Plus, the likelihood of her being snowed in for a while was great, and she really didn't want to shovel the driveway!

Sarah unlocked the cabin door and took the backpack off her back and the knife off of her hip. She gently removed Charlie from his sling and changed him. The walks they took seemed to make him tired every time – probably because there was so much to look at and it kept his little mind busy. She sat in the rocking chair on the porch and fed him until he fell asleep. She laid him on the bed in his little nest and prepared to get her pickles done.

While they were out for their walk, she had a large kettle of jars boiling over a fire outside. The water was no longer boiling, but it was still steaming hot. Charlie's wagon was lined with a towel and filled with cucumbers that Sarah had picked and washed that morning. From the cooler on the porch, she pulled out a large stock pan that contained cucumbers that she had cut into thick slices. She then salted and weighted them, along with some onions.

She had several fire pits going. One had a stockpot full of the syrupy liquid that she would pack her sliced pickles into, one had the canner filled with water, and another had a large pot of even more hot water, should she need it.

She fed all of the fires more wood to keep them burning nice and hot. She rinsed the cucumbers and onions well with cold water. While those drained over a large pot on the kitchen table, she quickly removed several jars from the hot water using a wooden spoon and a jar lifter. These she set into a cardboard box then covered them with a towel and quickly brought them into the cabin. She then carried the pickle syrup in and set it on the woodstove. Next she stirred the cucumbers and onions into the syrup mixture. Working quickly, she filled the hot jars and capped them with the canning lids and rims that were kept in a pan of hot water. She packed the filled jars back into the cardboard box, covered them with the towel, and carried them outside again. Carefully, she loaded the jars into the rack of the canner. She needed to add only a little more hot water to cover the tops of the jars. Replacing the canner lid, she set the timer,

127

which had come in a box of canning equipment, for 20 minutes.

As those pickles were processing, she got the next batch ready, then used much of the same process to make her dill pickles. The system worked out very well. She had canned some applesauce and apple pie filling the week prior; it was then that she came up with the notion of multiple fire pits. It was all well and good, as long as it wasn't windy. The fires beneath the pots were less effective in the wind and she was afraid of the jars bursting when pulling them out of the hot water. So she hoped for calm and still days to come until all of her canning was done. It was just too warm to do all of this inside of the cabin.

Charlie couldn't have timed his nap better. He awoke just as Sarah was pulling the last jar of dill pickles out of the hot water bath.

"Hello, Sweetheart," she said softly as she picked Charlie up. "Did you have a nice nap?"

Charlie was just beginning to smile and coo. Sarah loved to see his personality developing and although she loved cuddling with him as an infant, she was looking forward to his running around outside and talking to her. She already had been reading to him a few of the children's books that she had. He enjoyed the bright pictures and his mother's soothing voice.

They were sitting in the rocker on the porch when Sarah heard the familiar rumble of a pickup. "Listen, Charlie! Hank is coming!"

She set the book down on a large stump beside the chair, which she used as a table. With Charlie propped up against her chest, they watched for the truck to come into the clearing. Sarah was surprised to see two people in the truck. Then her heart started to pound. Henry had come along, too. Quickly, she started to assess if she looked okay. Her hair was up in a messy bun, she was in a pair of cutoff jeans and a T-shirt. Her skin was tan from being out in the sun all summer. With a sigh, she stood up to greet her guests. "What am I going to do, after all? Run into the cabin to fix myself up?" she thought.

She walked toward the truck to see what the two of them were untying in the pickup bed. Her eyes kept drifting back to Henry and his Levi's and white T-shirt. "Hidey, Sarah! Look what I found fer you!" Hank exclaimed.

"Hi, Hank. Hi, Henry."

"Hello, Sarah," said Henry, tipping his straw cowboy hat and giving her that award-winning smile. Sarah's heart thumped. She was sure that he could hear it. "Hi, Charlie! How are you, little guy?" Henry stroked Charlie's cheek softly with his index finger and Charlie smiled at him. Henry got a kick out of that.

"What's this, Hank?" Sarah asked, peeking into the pickup bed.

"A dresser! You said you wanted one fer the cabin. This was sittin' out at the end of Dalbec's driveway, waitin' to be taken. So I took it. It's a nice sturdy piece. I checked it out fer you. It will hold a lot; the drawers are nice and deep."

"Oh, Hank! Thank you!" said Sarah. "This is going to be perfect!"

"You go get the space ready where you want it; we're bringin' it in. Ready, Henry?"

"Ready."

The two men both gave a grunt with the initial lift of the dresser. Even though the drawers were out, it was still quite heavy. It didn't take Sarah long to clear a space and she pointed to the wall where she wanted it as they carried it into the cabin.

"If this had one more coat of varnish on it, it wouldn't have fit through the door! Heh-heh!"

Henry and Sarah laughed at Hank's observation. They placed the dresser up against the wall to the right of the door, centered beneath a window.

Charlie watched the activity from his stroller. Sarah took a rag and dusted it. It was a bulky oak piece with two drawers side by side on top, and three large single drawers below. It was in good shape, too. Sarah couldn't imagine why someone would just throw it away, but was glad that they did.

As Hank and Henry brought the drawers in, Hank told her, "We have to move it, Sarah."

"Why?"

"Because it has a mirror that attaches; it'll block the window."

They slid the dresser until it was centered between the window and the door, and then went to retrieve the mirror.

"Oh, Hank! I just love it! Thank you so much! And a mirror!" Sarah admired the dresser. The mirror was nearly as wide as the dresser itself and pivoted on two thick posts that held it in place.

"It will hold nearly everything you've got. Maybe more," said Hank.

Sarah felt her head drop a little, but then held it high again. True, she didn't have much, but she had what she needed and that was good enough for her. She knew Hank wasn't being snide; what he said was the truth. She was just a little embarrassed because Henry was there.

"You're right about that. I'll have everything put away in it today. Are you planning on fishing?"

"We thought we would if…" Hank started.

"Wait, Grandpa! There's one more thing in the truck for Charlie," Henry interrupted.

"Darn near forgot!" Hank clapped his hands together.

They went back out to the truck and carried something that was bundled up in thick quilts into the cabin. They set it on the floor.

"Open it, Sarah," Henry said with a bright smile. His eyes lit up with excitement.

Sarah looked at Hank. "What is it?"

"Jes' open it," replied Hank, shaking a finger at it.

Sarah knelt down beside the large bundle and untied the knots in the rope that held the quilts in place. She pulled back on the quilts to reveal what was inside.

"Hank! Henry! It's a crib!"

"Yep! It's the same crib my mother used for me."

"And my mother used it for me," Henry added.

Sarah was touched. "I'll take very good care of it. I promise." She was moved to tears. She had grown accustomed to sharing her bed with Charlie, and truly didn't mind, but she knew that sooner or later he wasn't going to lie so still and also that his napping on the bed could easily result in his falling onto the floor.

"Let's put it together, Grandpa." Henry was already kneeling down beside Sarah pulling the rails off the top of the stack.

It took them about 15 minutes to assemble the crib. The last step was laying the mattress down. Sarah went through the stack of towels and clothing that she had kept in a storage bin, smiling to herself because now she would store these items in her new dresser. She found what she was looking for. She wrapped a blanket around the mattress, then a sheet. It was a snug fit, but she was still able to get the mattress to lay flat on top of the spring frame of the crib.

Sarah stepped back. "Perfect! Hank, Henry, I just can't thank you enough." She gave them each a hug. Of course, she was certain that Henry could feel her heart pounding inside of her as she hugged him. She let go quickly, a bit flushed.

Henry smiled, "The look on your face is thanks enough..."

"Of course, we still want to go fishin' for our efforts, heh-heh," Hanked piped in.

13

Henry cast his line out into the water then sat down gently in the canoe. Hank glanced curiously over his shoulder to see where his grandson's cast had landed then looked back at his own bobber. The lake was calm and it quietly lapped at the sides of the canoe.

Occasionally, the call of a loon filled the air. The two men sat and fished without talking as they had done so many times since Henry was a small boy. However, it had been years since they were able to fish Lake Serene together. He loved this

lake as much as his grandfather did. The fishing
was great, but Henry thought it was more than that.
This land was so natural, so untouched. Pulling
down the driveway transported him to another
time. He could forget about the outside world and
truly live in the moment. Somehow, things like
crime, movie stars, politics just didn't exist in this
little world.

A fish jumped. By the time Hank and Henry
turned to see it, all that was left were ripples on the
water's surface. Once in a while, they were lucky
enough to see the fish, but most of the time, they
just heard a splash and saw the ripples.

"Why is she living out here, Grandpa?"
Henry broke the silence.

"No place else to go, I suppose." There was
no hesitation in Hank's response. It was as though
they were pondering the same thing.

"It just seems so extreme. To come way up
here, with a baby, and pretty much just live off the
land."

"It's been done before and proven to work."

"I know that, but it still just seems..." Henry
paused. "Where is Charlie's father?"

"I don't know, Henry. Then again, I never
asked. It just never seemed like the proper thing
to do."

Henry yanked his fishing pole back and stood up. Reeling the line, he said, "I just might need the net again!"

Hank turned and watched as Henry worked the fish closer and closer to the canoe, ready to grab the net if need be. A couple of times the fish jumped out of the water as it fought to get away.

"It's a big northern," Hank said. As it drew nearer, he gingerly leaned out to net it.

"Well, I think we have plenty for a couple of meals, at least," said Henry as he put the latest catch on the stringer. He held it up briefly to show two fairly good-sized northerns, four large sunnies, and a bass. Hank had caught a crappie earlier but threw it back because he would only eat crappies caught from ice fishing.

"I think you have a point there, Henry. Time to head back in."

Hank reeled in his line and threw the minnow from his hook into the lake. "Free food!" he said, "No strings attached! Heh-heh!"

The men took their positions and began to paddle back toward the cabin, leaving the stringer of fish in the water to be towed gently along.

"I'm going to ask her about Charlie's father," Henry stated after a while.

"Don't step on any toes, Henry." Hank warned.

"I won't. I'll be polite. Somehow."

"I don't see where it matters to you anyway."

"I want to get to know her better, Grandpa. Maybe even date her."

"Never knew you to date much."

"I rarely meet anybody that I feel like dating. So many of the girls around here are ditzy and they try to be something they're not. Sarah is different."

"She's a real special girl," Hank concluded.

14

Sarah sat outside on the porch in the rocking chair with a light blanket over her shoulders. Sipping her tea she let her shoulders relax. "Another long day," she thought. "And there is so much more to do." Softly, she began to cry. She missed her mother. She wanted her to see Charlie. She wanted Charlie to meet his grandma. "Oh, Mom, I am so tired. And I'm lonely for you," she said aloud. "I miss you."

She rocked and drank her tea while thinking of her mother. Even though Larry was her father, they never developed a relationship. She never felt as though she had a father, and always wished that she had. But her mother gave her so much love; she didn't have a need for Larry's affection. And now that she had Charlie, she knew how much her mother loved her.

Sarah straightened her head and wiped her tears. She must be as strong as her mother had been for her. There was just no other way. Her mother would come one day and see that Sarah and Charlie were just fine.

She stood up and carried her empty cup into the cabin. The woodstove was still warm from another day of canning beans. Tomorrow she would can more tomatoes. Sarah had to smile at all of the jars she had lined and stacked against the wall. Every day she became more confident that she would have enough food for the winter. Next year, she had already decided, her garden would be much larger. She definitely wanted more corn. She only got 12 pints of corn canned. She probably could have doubled that, but she enjoyed corn on the cob for dinner instead.

"Pop!" One of the lids on a jar of beans sealed. "Music to my ears," she thought as she closed the door for the night and locked it up. Hank had hung a screen door for her to help keep the flies and mosquitoes out. It sure did make a difference when she had the wood stove fired up. He also took measurements of all of her windows and was going to make screens for them. She could open the windows, but often didn't due to pesky insects.

Charlie stirred in his crib. It had taken him a couple of nights to get used to sleeping alone. Sarah missed having him right next to her, but they both slept better and longer. It was nearly nine o'clock and the sun was down for the night. Normally she would take advantage of the time that Charlie slept to get things done. Tonight, however, she just crawled into bed, exhausted.

15

The morning was quite cool and Sarah had actually used the heat in the car as they drove to town. It was Wednesday, and that meant that there would be an auction. She was hoping that there would be more canning jars, as she was running low and still had a considerable amount of tomatoes in the garden. September was just around the corner and with that, so was colder weather. The idea of winter made her both excited and nervous. She was certain that she could "hole up" for quite a while, as long as the pump didn't freeze up. But part of her worried that she was overlooking something that would not become obvious until the situation faced her.

As she pulled into the parking lot of the auction barn, she saw Hank's pickup and parked near it. She put Charlie in his stroller and tucked a small quilt around him. He had a knit hat that had little flaps and tie strings. The flaps covered part of his chubby cheeks when the strings were tied. Sarah also put socks over his hands to act as mittens. She didn't think he was overdressed for the weather, since he would be outside for an hour or so.

Hank spotted Sarah and Charlie as they came out of the number office.

"Hi-dee-ho!" he chirped. "Cold enough fer ya?"

"Morning, Hank!"

"Whatcha after today?"

"Canning jars, if I'm lucky," Sarah said.

"I didn't look for those, but there is a lot of stuff here today. The garage sales are coming to a halt and people are making a last effort to get rid of their junk."

"I better look around before they start, then."

There were a lot of chickens, ducks, geese, and turkeys. Sarah wouldn't mind having more, but she didn't have a place to keep them for the winter. She didn't know if the ones she already had were going to make it. However, Hank did bring over several bales of straw so Sarah could put the cage on top of them. That would keep them off the ground, at least. "Maybe next spring I'll see if Hank will build us a real chicken coop," she thought.

There were several lots with pots and pans, dishes, etc. Many of them had things like crockpots, blenders, items that were of no use to Sarah. One lot in the last row did intrigue her, however. It included a box of old hand tools, a box of a few electrical tools, and a box that had four railroad-style oil lamps. Sarah bent down to examine the lamps. A couple still had some oil in them. The other two looked like they would hold oil, but there was only one way to know for certain. There was a gallon and a half of lamp oil, a couple extra lamp glasses – one green, one red, and a box of wicks. She decided that this was one lot on which she would bid.

She heard the man with the microphone giving his test. She pushed Charlie over near the lot where they were beginning the auction and quickly scanned for jars. There were none in the first row. She slowed down a bit to look at the second row. There was one lot with about a dozen pints, but it also included a lot of other miscellaneous stuff she didn't need. At the end of the row she did find a small lot that had a box of jars – perhaps a couple dozen – some kitchen towels, hot pads, and cookbooks. She made a mental note of that lot and proceeded to look through the next row.

She spotted an item that caught her attention and pushed Charlie toward the plastic storage tub that had a teddy bear sticking out of the top. Looking into the tub, she saw it was filled with toys, books, and who knew what else.

The auctioneer was approaching the second row and he was heading toward a lot that Sarah wanted. She scurried over and became part of the bidding crowd. She got both of the lots for $5. She was pleased and headed back to the tub of toys and waited until the auctioneer and his posse made their way to it.

"We have a tub of toys here, and some other baby things," the auctioneer announced as the 16-year-old held up a toy telephone and the teddy bear.

"Who'll give me twenty?"

The crowd was still.

"Okay, then, let's start at fifteen."

There still was no reaction from the crowd and Sarah was glad.

The auctioneer peered down into the tub. "C'mon folks, there are books in here too. What sort of price are you going to put on your child's education?"

The crowd chuckled.

"Five dollars, then. Let's get this going. Who'll give me five?"

"Hep!"

Sarah looked around.

"I've got five, who'll give me six?"

Sarah held her number up.

"Hep!"

"Six. Who'll give me seven?"

"Hep!"

She was dismayed. She put the limit of ten dollars for this lot, confident that she'd get it.

"I've got seven, who'll give me eight?"

She flashed her number.

"Hep!"

"Eight. Eight. Who'll give me nine?"

"Hep!"

"I've got nine, do I hear ten?"

"Hep!"

"Eleven, eleven…"

"Hep!"

"Twelve, twelve…"

"Hep!"

"I've got twelve, do I hear thirteen?"

"Hep!"

"Thirteen, do I hear fourteen?"

Sarah held her card up.

"Hep!"

That was as high as she could go. She held her breath as the auctioneer continued, crossing her fingers that there would be no more bids.

"I've got fourteen, do I have fifteen? Fifteen…fifteen…" There was a long pause as the auctioneer and his helpers scanned the crowd for another bid.

"Hep!"

Sarah's heart dropped. For a moment she was certain that she had it. "I'm sorry, Sweetheart," she told Charlie. "Mommy tried."

Charlie looked up and smiled at her without a care in the world. This made her feel better, though she would have loved to have the toys for him.

"You win some, you lose some," came Hank's voice from behind.

"You can say that again," said Sarah. "I have one more lot that I want to bid on in the last row then I am done. Are you selling today?"

"Nope. Just watching."

Hank tagged along as Sarah headed to her next lot. He chuckled at the lot. "I don't think you'll have much competition with this one."

Sarah smiled, "That's the beauty of my necessities."

Hank chuckled again, "I like your attitude, Sarah."

16

Sarah and Charlie were out in the garden when Hank's pickup came rumbling through the trees. She picked up the potatoes she had just unearthed and added them to the pile in the wagon. Hank walked over to the garden.

"Quite the crop you got."

"Yes, it was a good gardening year, wasn't it?"

Hank nodded. "I brought your window screens fer you. I know it's a little late in the season, but early for next year, if you want to look at it that way!"

Sarah smiled. "Thank you so much, Hank. I do appreciate all you do for us."

"'Twas nothin'. Glad to do it," said Hank, being his modest self. He headed back toward his pickup and dropped the tailgate.

Sarah dropped her gloves on top of the potatoes in the wagon and pushed Charlie's stroller over to the pickup.

"How cold will it get in the root cellar during the winter, Hank?"

"Depends on how cold the winter is, heh-heh," he teased, then quickly added, "It will stay above freezing, so you can put your goods down there. That's what it was built for."

"That's a relief. I'm not complaining, but the kitchen area is filling up rapidly."

"You won't be starving this winter, that's fer sure. I'm real impressed, Sarah. All this work you do on your own. You've got ambition."

"I don't have much of a choice," Sarah replied.

Hank hung the screens by their hinges and left all of the windows open after he had finished. There was a light breeze that flowed though the cabin. Sarah thought ahead to the next year and how nice it would be to have this cross ventilation when the wood stove heated the cabin during the hot August canning season. There had been a few nights this year that were uncomfortably warm. Neither she nor Charlie slept well on those nights. If she opened the windows, then mosquitoes were a problem. Now, in mid-September, the nights were usually cool. The canning was nearly done, except for perhaps some more apples. She already had canned dozens of quarts and pints of applesauce and pie filling and also wrapped several individually for fresh eating. But there were still quite a few apples left on the trees. "Waste not, want not" is what came to mind.

Hank picked up Charlie and sat in the rocker on the porch with him. Sarah brought him out a glass of water and set it on the stump beside the rocker.

"You'd better put some sort of feet on yer little table here, or it'll eventually rot the flooring," said Hank observantly.

"I hadn't thought of that. I'll cut some from a branch and screw them on."

"Looks like yer near ready to hunker down for the winter."

"I think so. And after all this work, I'm ready to hunker down and rest."

Hank smiled at Charlie on his lap. "Now, how much rest do you think yer Mama's gonna git?"

Charlie smiled and cooed at Hank. "Yep. That's what I think, too," he responded.

Sarah smiled at the two of them. Charlie was getting so big. He was now five months old and starting to sit up. He loved eating his baby cereal from a spoon, as well as the homemade applesauce. Sarah had canned a special batch for him with nothing added to it, just plain apples and water.

"They say there are storms on the way. Should be in our area tomorrow morning," said Hank.

"Rainstorms?"

"Yep, with high winds and lightning."

Sarah stood up and walked toward the woodpile. She lifted a large rock from the end of the plastic tarp that she used to keep the wood dry, and pulled the tarp back. She stacked as much wood as she could carry in her arms and brought it into the cabin. She did this a few times then covered the wood pile up again, tightening the plastic and snuggling the rock up close to the base of the pile.

Then she picked up the rest of the potatoes that had already been dug up, brushed them off and added them to the wagon. The wagon was so full that a few of the vegetables fell over the tall sides as she pulled it toward the porch. "I'll have to put these out to dry more after the storm," she said. She went inside the cabin and came back out with several paper grocery bags. Gently, she packed the doubled up bags with potatoes and then brought them inside. She picked up the few that had dropped and added them to the fourth and last grocery bag, which was nearly half full.

"How much more do you have out there?" asked Hank.

"Oh, probably about 10 more plants worth."

She returned to the garden to gather her tools and gloves. She then took advantage of Hank's amusing Charlie to replenish the water in the reservoir, coffee pot, and any water jugs that were empty. Lastly, she gathered an armful of kindling and filled the kindling box. She sat down with Hank and Charlie and said, "Okay, it can rain now, if it wants."

"Not 'til I get home," said Hank, handing Charlie back to Sarah. Charlie's legs kicked with excitement as Sarah took him. They followed Hank out to his truck.

"Thank you again, Hank."

"You bet. Lock yer windows and it wouldn't be a bad idea to close the outside shutters, at least on the windows that aren't on the porch."

"I will. Wave bye-bye, Charlie." Sarah held Charlie's arm and made him wave to Hank as he backed his truck up and turned around. They watched his truck leave through the trees.

It was about three o'clock and time to feed Charlie and let him nap. He'd been up since eleven o'clock a.m. and was beginning to yawn. Sarah fed and changed him then sat in the rocker on the porch, where he fell asleep quickly in her arms.

17

While Charlie slept in his crib, Sarah opened the door to the root cellar and began bringing all of her canned goods down the ladder. In the beginning, it was slow and tedious. Then she came up with the idea of loading one of the plastic milk crates that she got from an auction with as many jars as she could lift and lowered them down into the cellar using some of the clothes line she had left over. It was still slow going, but it was certainly more expedient than carrying three or four jars at a time down the ladder.

It took nearly two hours to get the canned goods moved and arranged on the shelves. She set the last jar of jelly on the shelf then stood back and smiled. All of the shelves were nearly full. She decided, too, that she would buy yet another plastic storage bin to store the bags of flour, sugar, and other dry goods she'd need for the winter.

Sarah glanced at the trunk that contained the personal items of her family. She had yet to open it, but promised herself that she would someday. Climbing back up the ladder, she blew the lantern out and closed the heavy door in the floor. She could hear and feel the wind picking up a bit. Following Hank's advice, she closed the outside shutters of the cabin leaving the one on the window facing the porch open. The cabin was quite dark, so Sarah lit a couple of lanterns. She hung one from a log rafter above the table. The other she kept on the dresser in front of the mirror.

She walked out onto the porch and scanned the perimeter for anything that may need to be brought into the cabin before the rain came. The wind became stronger and the chickens scurried into their nesting boxes. Sarah lifted the heavy rocking chair and set it near the woodstove. She locked the screen door with the eye and hook then closed the strong wooden door to the cabin and locked that too.

Charlie was lying awake in his crib watching her as she closed the porch window even though it wasn't necessarily cool. After starting a fire in the woodstove, she picked Charlie up and put him in his car seat on the table so he could watch her as she made their dinner. Tonight it was a baked potato, salad, and some fresh green beans.

Sarah didn't get very much sleep that night. She listened to the wind howl through the trees and the rain pour loudly on the roof. Amazingly, Charlie slept quite soundly. But Sarah felt the need to be prepared to get down into the cellar should there be a tornado. She didn't really feel there would be, but it was just so windy and loud. She already had the table moved to the side, off of the cellar door, just in case.

Inside the cabin it was warm and cozy. She kept a small fire going in the woodstove and kept the lantern on the dresser burning dimly.

She slept on and off for about an hour at a time. Either a branch dropping on the roof or a loud clap of thunder would wake her. Around five o'clock, however, it was something else that got her up. She thought she had heard a whimpering near the door. She stood motionless trying to discern what she was hearing amid the noise of the storm, which was now dying down.

Too frightened to open the door and look out, she pressed her cheek up to the glass of the porch window to try to get a glimpse of what could possibly be out there. The stump that she kept near the rocking chair obstructed her view. It was still dark outside, but occasionally a flash of lightning lit up the porch. Still, she saw nothing. She closed the inside shutter on the window then walked over to the door and knelt down. This time she put her ear to the door and listened hard. At times she thought she'd heard something, and then she'd doubt herself thinking it was probably just the storm.

"If there is something out there," she warned herself, "it could be a raccoon, or a skunk, or even a bear!" She poked at the fire and added another small log before she climbed back into bed.

18

Sarah ended up sleeping until nearly eight o'clock a.m., which was when Charlie began to fuss. She sat up and rubbed her eyes. The cabin was still dark because all of the shutters were closed. The lamp was still burning dimly on the dresser. She opened the shutters on the porch window. The storm had passed. She poked at the remaining embers in the woodstove and added wood to it. She changed and fed Charlie then sat and rocked with him near the warm stove. Full and dry, he was now content to sit in his car seat.

She looked out again onto the porch through the window. She did not see nor hear anything. "It must have been just my imagination," she said aloud to Charlie as she began to unlatch the cabin door.

Pulling the door open, she stepped back in surprise. Up against the screen door, there was a black puppy. He was sleeping soundly but rose to his feet when Sarah opened the door.

"Where did you come from?" Sarah exclaimed. She opened the screen door and stepped out onto the porch. The puppy came right up to her. She could not imagine where he had strayed from. "You must be hungry," she said, stooping down to pick him up.

She brought him into the cabin and lined a milk crate with a large towel. After setting the puppy down on the towel, she began to make some oatmeal. She made twice as much as she normally would, hoping that the puppy would eat it.

The warm cabin felt good to the puppy. He was chilled from the wet, cold night he had spent on the porch. Sarah looked down at him, sorry that she hadn't been brave enough to open the door at five o'clock a.m. when she had first heard him whimpering.

"But you're okay now," she resolved, "and a belly full of warm food will make you feel as good as new!" She spooned the oatmeal into two bowls and poured milk over each of them. She lifted the puppy out of the crate and set him near his bowl on the floor. He sniffed at the contents and quickly began to eat.

Sarah was only half finished with her oatmeal when the puppy was licking his bowl clean. She was relieved that he had eaten it. While she finished her breakfast, the puppy sniffed around the cabin, checking things out.

Sarah guessed that he must be about four or five months old, as he was past the round, bouncy stage and his legs were a bit long. He was all black with short hair and large feet. He had no collar. He also appeared to be a bit thin to Sarah. "You must have been lost for days," she said, petting him.

She bundled Charlie up and put him in his stroller. The morning was damp and cool. The puppy immediately jumped up putting his big paws on Charlie's lap. Sarah quickly reprimanded him and told him "No!" in a very stern voice. The puppy cowered for a bit but learned the lesson. The three of them went outside. The shutters were opened in order to allow the brightness of the morning sun into the cabin.

Sarah looked around the area. There were several branches scattered about that had broken off from the strong winds. She checked on the chickens, and found herself reprimanding the pup once again.

The garden was quite wet. She knew she'd have to get the remainder of the onions, carrots, potatoes, and garlic up soon. They still needed to be dried in the sun somewhat before she brought them down to the cellar for winter storage.

As she began to pull up some of the crops, the puppy ran about sniffing and exploring. He would disappear into the woods for perhaps five minutes, and then come back to Sarah and Charlie as though to make sure they hadn't left him.

19

The sky was blue and the sun was warm for the next several days. Sarah was relieved. She had the last of her root crops dug up and she spread them out on two quilts in the sun for drying. She turned them every now and then so they'd cure evenly.

The puppy had learned very quickly that he was not to mess with Charlie. However, the chickens were a different story. He nearly caught one the day before. Sarah had tied him to a tree in the woods, away from the cabin, for an hour as a punishment. When she went to retrieve him, he walked obediently at her side. "He is learning," she thought.

Today Sarah braided the onion and garlic tops and hung them in the root cellar. She filled milk crates with the carrots, which would allow air circulation and prevent rot. For the potatoes, she had to make a crate. She gathered many straight branches, peeled the bark from them, and allowed them to dry. Then she made the bottom of the crate by laying five of the sturdier branches down. Crossing these with shorter branches in the opposite direction, she fastened them with nylon twine. She spaced them so that the potatoes would not fall through. Four sides were made in the same manner and she assembled all five parts into a large crate. She set the crate on some logs on the cellar floor.

Grocery bag by grocery bag, she hauled the potatoes down. The crate was soon filled to its capacity. It was now October and the cold weather had approached for the winter. Occasionally there would be a sunny, mild day. But for the most part, the temperatures were around 40 degrees. Sarah had an ample supply of wood, thanks to Hank. He had taught her all about using the chainsaw, though he did not like the idea of her using it when she was alone.

She was sitting at the table reading through her indispensible cookbook when she heard Hank pull in. The puppy ran up to the truck, growling and barking. Both Hank and Henry stepped out, not deterred by the watchdog. Henry squatted down. "Where did you come from?" he asked the pup, who was now no longer barking but wagging his tail as Henry scratched behind his ears.

"He came to us during that last big storm," Sarah called from the porch.

Henry picked up a stick and threw it. The puppy chased after it and brought it back to him, Hank was dropping his tailgate, as he usually did when he visited Sarah.

"C'mon, Henry. No time for play."

"What's up?" asked Sarah.

"We were getting our houses ready for winter, and came up with a good idea for yers," Hank explained. "We want to wrap the porch with this plastic. It will make a big difference, I'm sure. If nothing else, it'll keep the snow off the porch."

"That sounds like a great idea!" Sarah said.

The two men went right to work. They first took the thick plastic film and attached it just beneath the roofline on the northern edge of the porch. Then they pulled it as snug as they could against the cabin's uneven log wall and attached it there. They did likewise along the bottom, just beneath the porch floor. The plastic turned the corner and they affixed it to the first porch post where the steps began. Here, they cut the plastic and hung a screen door. They had already covered the door with plastic on both sides. They kept working until the entire porch was enclosed. Then they re-enforced where the plastic was stapled with lath and nails.

Sarah kept the puppy inside with her while they worked. She had vegetable soup made when they finished, and they were thankful.

"It's getting plenty cold today," said Hank as he came inside. "I bet we see single digits once the sun goes down."

Henry spotted a roll of paper towels and took one to blow his nose, politely turning his back to Sarah as he did so.

Sarah's heart pounded like it usually did when he was nearby. She tried not to stare at him. Henry lifted the firebox door that was on the top of the wood stove surface and threw in the paper towel. Then he took the liberty of rousing the fire and adding another log.

"It smells good in here, Sarah," he said, smiling.

"It's vegetable soup."

"All fresh veg, I suppose." Henry picked the puppy up. "So, where did this little guy come from?"

"I don't know, he was on my porch the morning after that big storm. He was cold and hungry, so I took him in and fed him. He's been here ever since."

"I think the Good Lord felt you needed a watchdog," Hank said.

"Maybe so," said Sarah. "I just hope someone out there isn't missing their puppy."

"My guess is that he was abandoned. You have two neighbors, and they're each more than a mile away. If it belonged to one of them, they would have stopped here by now to see if you found him." Hank always sounded reasonable.

"Who would just abandon a puppy like that?" Sarah was disgusted.

"Sadly, there are people like that," Hank concluded.

"What's his name?" Henry asked.

"So far, 'Puppy.' I just haven't found one that fits yet."

"That's a pretty soft name for a tough looking guy like this," Henry said, setting the puppy down. "How about Puppenstein?"

They all laughed at Henry's absurd suggestion.

171

"I think I'll mull over a few others first. Come, sit down and have some soup."

Hank and Henry each had two bowls of soup, along with some crackers and milk. Sarah had put some soup in what was now the puppy's dish, along with some torn pieces of bread. He ate it right up. She was certain that he was getting enough to eat at this point because he was putting on weight. But he was only going to eat more as he grew and Sarah hadn't figured on cooking for three all winter.

While the men ate, Sarah changed and fed Charlie. Afterwards, she was sitting in the rocker in front of the wood stove when Henry reached his hands out and scooped up Charlie.

"Hey, big boy! How are you?" Charlie smiled and drooled on Henry's shirt. "That good, huh?" He laughed.

"He's ready to pop a tooth through," said Sarah.

"Then you can have a drumstick at Thanksgiving," joked Henry.

Henry just loved Charlie. What was more, he loved Sarah, too. But he was uncertain how to approach her as far as dating went. He assumed dating would always include Charlie, and that was fine with him. He just didn't know how she would react. He also didn't know what the situation was between Sarah and Charlie's father. Henry wasn't giving up the idea of dating, but he was going to take it very slowly. They were getting closer and more comfortable with each other as time went on, and this helped him pace himself.

Sarah watched Henry with Charlie. "He is so good with him," she thought. Sarah loved Henry, but didn't know if he felt the same way about her. She knew he liked her. He was always kind to her, and caring. But so was Hank, and perhaps it was just the Jacobson genes.

"I'll be right back," Hank interrupted both Henry's and Sarah's thoughts. He went outside letting a cold waft of air in as he opened the door.

Henry felt like blurting out quickly how he felt about Sarah while his grandfather had gone outside. He was trying to think of something to say that would let her know of his interest in her in a way that wouldn't scare her off, so to speak. What he felt like saying is "I love you!" at the top of his lungs. "C'mon, Henry, think, think!" he thought to himself. He was now in the rocker with Charlie, and Sarah was clearing the table.

She looked at Henry, "A penny for your thoughts."

Henry's head turned slowly up and he looked at her eyes. He was scrambling to arrange his thoughts knowing this was a perfect opportunity to tell her how he felt, but didn't know what to say. Then it came to him.

"Sarah…" he began.

Whoosh! The door opened and Hank quickly closed it. "Wind's pickin' up," said Hank. "Here, Sarah, I got you a couple of presents." Hank pulled a gadget from the box he had retrieved from his truck.

"What is it?" asked Sarah.

"It's a radio, only it don't take 'lectricity. An' you don't need no batteries. You jes' crank it up and that puts a charge on it." He cranked the radio and tuned it in to the local news station. "If you crank it for a couple minutes, you'll get about 15 minutes of radio. You can pick up a few TV stations, too. An' over 'ere is a light."

"This is really something, Hank! What will they think of next?!"

Hank chuckled thinking how it wasn't exactly new technology. He reached back into the box. "An' this is just a flashlight. Shake it for three minutes and you'll get about 20 minutes of light. Good for outside."

Sarah hugged Hank and kissed him on the cheek. "Thank you! Thank you both for putting up the plastic and for these things!" Sarah was excited to be able to listen to the radio without having to sit in her car.

Henry smiled. "You're welcome, Sarah."

"Oh, Henry, you were going to tell me something. What was it?" Sarah asked.

Henry looked at her softly. This time their eyes locked and Sarah felt he was trying to tell her something important.

"Storm. I think you should name the puppy 'Storm,'" he said.

Sarah looked at him, then at the puppy, then back at Henry.

"Yes. That is a good name. We'll name him Storm." She continued to look at Henry's gaze, knowing that was not what she was paying him a penny for.

20

Sarah loved having the porch enclosed. Now as she split wood, she stacked it inside the porch. It would keep dry and was very accessible. This pleased her. She also took some of the leftover plastic and enclosed the chickens' cage. On sunny days it would warm up nicely for them. The cage now had a solid floor of straw bales, and bales stacked up along the sides and back of the nesting box. There were also two more on top. Sarah had to move one of them in order to feed and water them, but she didn't mind. She just hoped they'd make it through the winter. The hens stopped laying some time ago and Sarah really missed having fresh eggs to collect daily.

Storm had grown quite a bit in the past month and was learning his place very quickly. He'd bark when he heard critters outside of the cabin and scare them off. He no longer pestered the chickens, although they were always penned up now. He was very gentle around Charlie and just a plain good dog. A good, *hungry* dog. Sarah had to cook for three now to keep up with his appetite. She was going to town today and planned to get a large bag of dog food for him.

Henry tuned up her car for the winter. He told her to keep the tank at least half full and to be certain to start it up and let it run a good long time on cold days.

Today it was only about 15 degrees outside, according to the oversized outdoor thermometer. According to the news, it was 18 degrees with a wind chill of 10 degrees. Not a bad day to get some errands done. It was supposed to snow in a couple of days – eight inches in some areas. Sarah bundled Charlie up and put him in his car seat. He was now too big for the carrier so she had traded it in at a second-hand store for a walker and a highchair. It wasn't an even trade, but she only had to pay $15 more for the two items. The new car seat, on the other hand, had cost her nearly $60, but it would last for several years.

Sarah pulled out of the driveway and onto the road, which was clear of ice and snow. So far this season there had only been about an inch of snowfall in this area, and that inch came on two separate days.

Her first stop was the Laundromat. She threw in a large load, which again consisted mainly of diapers, and waited until she was able to put them in the dryer. At the grocery store, she purchased four of each 10-pound bags of flour and sugar, as well as other baking needs such as soda, powder, and salt. She threw in several bags of frozen bread dough, as this was the cheapest way for her to buy bread and now that it was so cold out, the whole world was her freezer! She took advantage of this but still grabbed four more jugs of water. She needed them for storage of drinking water since she had been letting a couple of the jugs at home freeze for use in the coolers where she kept things like milk, eggs, cheese and other perishables handy. The grocery bill came to almost $70, but the bulk of her purchase would last for several months.

She went to the butcher shop next and bought some soup bones, meat scraps, and a large slab of bacon. Hank told her that the butcher at this shop was a fair man and that this would be the cheapest way to buy meat. Sarah would have to sort through the meat scraps and cut off any fat that she didn't want, and then pack it herself. The bacon, which she had the butcher slice, would be packed into individual servings. She knew that Storm would just love the soup bones, after she made the soup, of course. These, too, had quite a bit of meat on them. She placed the meat into the trunk and proceeded to the grain elevator for dog food and chicken feed. This was another tip from Hank.

With her tank full of gas and her warm load of laundry in the back seat next to Charlie, they headed home.

They were gone for 2 ½ hours. The wood on the fire had been reduced to embers, but the cabin was still warm and the embers were hot enough to get the freshly added logs burning.

Sarah let Storm out to run around for a while. He would always sniff at the circumference of the cabin and make sure everything was okay. Sometimes he'd run down to the lake, but he would not walk on the ice. It had not yet frozen completely over.

Storm loved to be outside. He often spent most of the day outside, and on colder days, he was more content to lie on his quilt that Sarah kept on the porch for him than he was to be inside the warm cabin. This was fine by Sarah, as Charlie was beginning to really enjoy his time in his walker and she preferred the dog outside.

Charlie loved to sit up and scoot in his walker, but the soft socks on his feet hindered his ability to move about. He also enjoyed playing with the colorful toys that were attached to the tray in front of him.

While Charlie played in his walker, and Storm played outside, Sarah sat by the table and worked on some sewing. She folded Storm's quilt in half and stitched the sides together. She had been working on this for a couple of days now and was nearly finished. She left about 20 inches unstitched then pulled the quilt through the opening so her stitches were inside. Taking some straw, she stuffed it quite full then stitched up the opening. This was Storm's new bed for the porch. He would be much warmer and more comfortable on this thick nest. She set the bed down on the porch and opened the screen door.

"Storm! Come here, Storm!" she called and gave a couple of whistles. Within moments the large puppy came into the porch. His dark coat was speckled with white. It was beginning to snow.

Sarah put Charlie in his crib and gathered up all of the water jugs. She topped off the reservoir to its brim, as well as the large enamelware coffee pot. Putting the empty jugs and water bottles into the

181

wagon, she pulled it into the woods to the pump. Storm stayed on the porch to guard the cabin.

Hank and Henry had built a small building around the pump, and stacked straw bales around the sides of it. She opened the door and stepped inside. The water was very cold these days. After she filled all of her containers, she made certain that the water had slowed to a trickle and closed up the pump house. As she pulled the wagon back to the cabin, it began to snow harder and the ground was turning white.

She put the water inside on the floor along the wall and lifted the wagon up into the porch. Storm had cuddled up on his new bed and didn't make any effort to get up, so Sarah latched the porch door then went inside the cabin.

The time was four o'clock and it was starting to get dark. Sarah lit the lantern above the table, as well as the lantern on the dresser. The two of them lit the cabin nicely, but it wasn't bright by any means. When she felt she needed more light, she could turn the wicks up or light the other lanterns that hung from the beam ceiling.

The cabin smelled good. She had made a large batch of vegetable beef and barley soup. After ladling a portion into a bowl, she set the stockpot with the remainder of it on the table to cool. She was excited to have such a hearty meal. The soup bone was now cool and she gave it to Storm, who took it eagerly and lay back in his bed and began to chew on it. Sarah could hear the faint hollow noise through the thick log wall as his teeth clacked on the bone.

She had also baked a couple dozen dinner rolls that she made by thawing out some frozen bread dough and setting two small balls of it in each division of a cupcake pan. She bagged up most, but set three of them in one side of the bun warmer on the wood stove.

Everyone ate like kings that evening. Even Charlie had a small amount of soup! By seven o'clock, Charlie was more than ready to go to bed. His belly was full of warm soup and milk. Sarah hugged and kissed him good night then tucked him into his crib. She added as many logs to the fire as she could, turned out the lanterns, and climbed into bed herself. It felt good to lie down and rest.

As they often did, her thoughts turned to her mother. Wondering how she was doing and when she would see her again. She so badly wanted her to meet Charlie. She so badly just wanted to hug her. Before Sarah had left the morning of April eighteenth, her mother stressed the importance of patience and that they may not see each other for years. It hopefully would be sooner, but it still may not be for years. It would take planning and time in order for Joan to get away from Larry in a manner where she wouldn't have to worry about him following her.

"I want to be free of him forever, Jill," she told her. "And that may take some time."

"Jill" was Sarah's name given at birth. At first it was difficult to get used to being called Sarah, but since meeting Hank, she became accustomed to it.

Sarah continued to think about her mother until she drifted off to sleep. Her pillow was damp with tears.

21

It was still snowing at five o'clock a.m. when Sarah got up for the day. She poked at the fire and added logs, impressed with how warm the stove kept the cabin. She opened the door and looked at Storm. He was curled up on his bed and content. Unlocking the screen door, she asked, "Do you wanna go out?" Storm perked his head up. It was still dark outside, but the air smelled different to him. He stood up and stretched. Walking slowly to the door, he stuck his nose out and sniffed. He stepped out into the snow, looked around, and made his routine check of the cabin's perimeter.

Sarah lit the railroad lantern that hung from the ceiling on the porch. Taking a shovel, she cleared the steps and a small area on the ground in front of the porch. It had already snowed about 10 inches. She wondered how much more they would get.

Leaving Storm outside, she filled his dog food dish and brought the now frozen pail of water into the cabin to thaw. Storm had two water pails. Sarah switched them with one another as they froze.

This morning she had bacon, eggs, and a couple of dinner rolls for breakfast, along with some orange juice and a vitamin. As she often did these days, she listened to the radio while she had her breakfast. The snow was predicted to continue until noon. She decided that she would shovel paths to the chickens, the woodpile, the pump house, and the outhouse even before the snow stopped. She knew she would have to shovel again, but thought shoveling twice would be quicker and easier.

It was a light fluffy snow and shoveling was not the chore it could have been. And Sarah was glad, even though shoveling a bit of heavy snow would hold no threat to her, as her body had become quite lean and strong since she moved to the cabin in the woods.

Storm romped about in the deeper banks. He would stick his face in the snow then pull it out and look at Sarah. She had to laugh at the sight of his white face and dark eyes and nose. He truly loved the outdoors and was a very happy dog. Sarah was glad and thankful that he came to them that stormy night. He belonged here.

The days were long and dark. Sarah spent a lot of her time reading, both to herself, and to Charlie. On mild days she would take him outside and pull him around in his "sled," which was a short plastic storage bin with a length of rope tied to it.

Charlie loved to be outside. Storm enjoyed the company as well. She would pull him over to look at the chickens, although they weren't easily visible through the clouded plastic. Sometimes they would go down to the lake or out in the woods where deer trails were abundant. It was not unusual to see a herd of 20 or more deer in the clearing near the lake.

On this particular day, it was too cold to have Charlie outside. While he napped, she went out to the pump house to fill the water jugs. As the last jug was placed in the sled, which she now used in place of the wagon, Storm ran toward the cabin, barking. It wasn't his usual bark. Sarah stopped and listened. She didn't hear anything. "Why did Storm take off like that?" she wondered. She walked toward the cabin. Storm was still barking, but he stopped in front of the steps that led up to the porch. There was a vehicle that Sarah didn't recognize parked behind her car. Sarah slowed down just as she approached the edge of the woods. A dense blue spruce helped to hide her. She could see the fur on Storm's back rise as he continued to bark. Something was wrong. It was obvious to her that he was protecting Charlie by standing in front of the porch door. Sarah's heart began to pound. She started running to the cabin then suddenly stopped.

"Hey!" A voice called from behind a dark ski mask. Sarah screamed and turned to run toward the woodpile where her splitting maul was in the stump. It was difficult to run through the snow and the oversized boots on her feet seemed to weigh a ton.

Her mind began to fill with the most dreadful of thoughts. Larry had found her! They'll take Charlie! She muscled her way through the untouched drifts toward the woodpile.

"Go away!" she screamed. She could now hear a man's voice yelling at her but she couldn't understand what he was saying. She didn't care.

She just wanted to get to that maul and protect Charlie.

He was getting closer. Sarah's chest seized with pain as she inhaled the subzero air. She stumbled and fell. Something tugged at the heel of her boot. Kicking and scrambling to her knees, then back to her feet, she ran again. The woodpile was only about 10 feet away. Her arms reached to it, willing the splitting maul to come to her. Then she felt herself fall. The man had a hold of both of her legs.

"Let me go! Let me go!" Sarah was screaming and crying. The man held her down in the snow as he climbed up her body and was now completely on top of her, with his arms around her shoulders. She was face down in the snow and helpless. Though she continued to struggle and scream, she could not break the man's grip.

"Go away! Go away! Go away!"

The man turned her over onto her back. Her eyes were wide with fear as she looked at the obscured face. All she could see were his eyes and his mouth. Her head dropped back and she lay limp in the snow, passed out from exhaustion.

22

When Sarah woke up, she found herself tucked in her bed. "It was all a dream," she thought, relieved.

She heard Charlie babbling, but it wasn't coming from his crib. Sitting upright quickly, she saw him sitting on the lap of a figure in front of the stove. He stood and carried Charlie toward her then placed him in his crib. Sitting beside her on the bed, he asked, "Are you okay?"

Sarah was confused. "What's going on?"

"Don't you remember? You were out at the pump house getting water when I got here. You ran from me…what's the matter, Sarah?" Henry had one hand on her shoulder and was tenderly lifting her chin so she would look at him.

"Oh, Henry!" She couldn't say anything, but just sobbed on his shoulder. Henry let her cry it out, holding her close in his arms.

"Shhh…" he consoled, and stroked her head with his strong hand. "Shhh…"

Sarah told him everything. She told him about Larry, the commune, Charlie's father, her mother, the escape. All of it. The relief she felt was so great that it surprised her. It surprised Henry, too. Though it did answer many of his questions, he was not expecting this.

"Henry, I'm sorry. I'm sorry that I've gotten you involved with this. I didn't mean to. It was so nice the day I met Hank. He has helped me out so much, and his company kept me going. Then meeting you…"

"I'm not sorry, Sarah." Henry held her face in his hands and looked into her tear-drained eyes. His heart was pounding. He wondered if he should tell her how he felt. His heart felt that he should just say, "I love you," but his mind was telling him that this was not the time. "Come and get something to eat. I made stew for you." He stood up and patted Charlie's head as he walked back to the wood stove.

Sarah watched him. She wondered if she had done the right thing by telling him of her history. She pulled the quilts off of her lap. She was wearing a sweater and long johns. Embarrassed, she pulled on her jeans then picked up Charlie and gave him a tight hug. She walked to the stove with her son in her arms.

"Henry," she said softly. Henry turned and looked at her. "How long have I been sleeping?"

"Nearly two days."

Sarah looked around. The water jugs were in the cabin, the wood box was full, and there was a rolled up quilt on the floor near the dresser. He had stayed here all this time and had taken care of Charlie.

"Thank you, Henry."

Henry smiled and placed a bowl of stew on the table. "It's the least I could do. After all, I'm the one that caused all of this."

Sarah looked puzzled.

"If I hadn't scared the daylights out of you, you would have been just fine," he explained.

Sarah sat down and ate the stew. It was very good, but something about it was different. It was unlike anything she had had before.

"What kind of stew is this?"

"Rabbit. Snared one yesterday. You have a ton of them around here."

She shared a few bites with Charlie, who was now eager to eat anything, but at seven months, he didn't have the luxury of molars to indulge in anything much past the mushy stage.

They talked while Charlie scooted about in his walker. Sarah had found some little shoes for him that allowed him to push his way around the cabin floor. She now had to block off the woodstove so he wouldn't get burned.

Their conversation was different now. Henry asked Sarah a few questions about where and how she grew up. She answered him with all honesty and appreciated how he seemed to accept her past.

He told her that the reason he had come out here was to invite her and Charlie to his family's Thanksgiving dinner. The jeep he was using was his mother's. He was surprised, actually saddened, that Sarah had never celebrated Thanksgiving, nor Christmas. Her mother had told her about holidays and as much as she could about God. She even had a tiny Bible that she kept hidden from Larry. Every once in a while, they would go for walks and sit out in a field and her mother would read to Sarah and explain to her about religion. This was just something they simply were not allowed to discuss within the commune. While Larry did hold meetings where he "preached," it was all about Mother Earth and the evils of Man.

"I'd be happy to bring you and Charlie to church each week, if you'd like."

"Can I do that? I mean, I don't exactly belong..."

"Everybody is welcome, Sarah," he said.

Charlie pushed his walker up to Henry. "Hey, Buddy!" Henry picked him up. "I bet you're tired. You've been up for quite a while."

"I'll change him..." Sarah began.

"I've got it," said Henry.

Sarah smiled and didn't object. She fed some more wood to the fire and made some tea. Charlie lay right down, babbled for a few minutes, then fell asleep.

Henry cranked up the radio and turned it to a station that was playing Christmas music.

"May I have this dance?" He extended his hand toward Sarah.

Sarah put her hand in his and stood up. "But I don't..."

"Shhh..." He pressed a finger to her lips and then took her in his arms. They rocked back and forth gently while "O, Holy Night" played.

Sarah had her head on Henry's chest. Henry held Sarah's hand and had one arm wrapped around her waist. He pressed his cheek against her head, closed his eyes and enjoyed the moment.

23

For the next few Sundays, Henry had come out to pick up Sarah and Charlie for church. Disapproving looks from some of the people made Sarah feel awkward as they walked in, but Henry stood tall and confident. This helped her keep her own head up. "Don't worry about it," he had told her. However, Henry couldn't help but to feel a little betrayed by some of the parishioners. People who he had always gotten along well with now seemed to think that Henry had something to be ashamed of.

"They'll come around, Henry, then feel like fools," his grandfather told him. "People assume, then rumors start. Jes' don't fret about it."

Henry kept this in mind, because his grandfather never steered him wrong. But it was still hurtful.

On the Sunday before Christmas, Henry wanted Sarah to meet his family. They were meeting at a restaurant in Long Creek Falls. Sarah was both eager and nervous. She had heard many stories about his family and was certain they'd get along fine, but still, she was nervous.

During the ride to town, Sarah asked, "Henry, exactly how much does your family know about me?"

Henry knew what she was driving toward. "Well, they know you're a Brenny, that you live on Lake Serene with your son, Charlie, and they know that you are very special to me and Grandpa."

Henry could feel Sarah still looking at him. "As for all the things you've told me," he continued, "about what brought you out here to begin with, I've kept that in confidence."

Sarah let out a deep breath and looked out her window. Henry reached over and patted her hand.

"Very special," Sarah mulled the words over in her mind. "I wonder what he means by that?"

198

"Here we are!" Henry shifted the Jeep into "park." He always borrowed his mom's car when he had Sarah and Charlie along because the cab space in his pickup didn't accommodate two adults and a car seat very well.

Sarah got Charlie out and walked along the sidewalk with Henry's hand at her elbow. Even here, in Long Creek Falls, the three of them got odd looks. Still, Henry would tip his hat to the ladies and greet people politely.

They were almost to the restaurant when somebody called out, "Hey, Jacobson! Where'd you get the family?" Henry's stride slowed only slightly, his grip on Sarah's elbow tightened a bit has he urged her forward. He didn't respond, but did look in the direction of where the voice came from as he held the door open for Sarah and Charlie. He knew very well whose comment that was. It was Bob McCarthy. He had grown up and gone to school with him, and as far as Henry could tell, he would never change. Bob was the kid that was always mouthing off and getting into trouble. "A boy that will never be a man," Henry thought as the restaurant door closed behind him.

24

A woman walked up to Henry and said, "Oh good! You're here!" Henry kissed her cheek.

"Mom, this is Sarah. Sarah, this is my mom, Grace."

"Oh, I am so happy to meet you finally! You know, Henry and his grandfather have talked so much about you and...ohhh! This must be Charlie! Oh, may I?" she asked Sarah as she took Charlie from her arms. "My, aren't you a handsome boy!

Come back here, you two. We reserved the back room."

Sarah watched as Grace walked away with Charlie. She looked at Henry, who just smiled and said, "That's Mom!"

They stepped into the dining room. "Everyone, this here is Charlie," Grace announced. Calls came from the table.

"Hey, Charlie!"

"Chuck!"

"Oh, he's adorable!"

"And this is Sarah," Grace continued.

"Hi, Sarah! Nice to meet you!"

"Hey, Sarah!"

"Now you sit here, and we have a highchair for Charlie. Will he sit up, Dear?" Grace continued.

Sarah smiled. "Yes, he will. Thank you," she said and laughed to herself because she wasn't sure if it mattered what she would have said, as Grace already had Charlie halfway into the highchair.

Grace was a high-spirited, petite lady of about five foot two, with dark hair cut just above her shoulders and her eyes were round and bright blue, just like Henry's.

Sarah sat down as instructed, and Henry sat at the head of the table on the opposite side of Charlie. Sarah looked around her at the busy atmosphere. Everyone was chatting up a storm.

Two waitresses bustled around the table getting water for everyone and passed out menus.

"Okay, everyone! Grandpa, Jake, and John are here," Grace said.

Hank walked in first. "Hidey, hidey!" he said and sat at the head of the table opposite Henry. He winked at Sarah. Following him came two tall men. Their broad frames made the room feel smaller. One of the men sat next to Sarah. He looked at her and smiled. "Name's John. How do you do?"

Sarah shook his hand. "I'm Sarah," she said.

The other man sat across the table from her and gave Sarah a nod and a smile. Grace put her hands on his shoulders. "Sarah, this is Sam. Henry's dad."

"Hello, Sarah." His voice was low and strong. "Everyone just calls me Jake." He extended his hand across the table.

Sarah put her hand in his massive paw. "Nice to meet you," she said softly. Big Jake was a very handsome man who stood six foot four, with dark, golden hair and hazel eyes. Many people who had met him said he looked like Clint Eastwood.

Grace closed the long accordion door that separated their dining room from the rest of the restaurant. "Everybody, listen up! You all know who Sarah and Charlie are…" They all stopped talking and looked at Grace. "Sarah, this is John," she started next to Sarah. "Henry's uncle, and his wife, Clare. Then we have Jessica and Steve, Henry's aunt and uncle, and their daughter, Lisa. They have a son, Paul, but he couldn't make it." Now Grace was standing behind Hank. "Of course, you know Grandpa," and continued from the corner of the table opposite Sarah. "These two are Little John and Jimmy, Henry's cousins. And Joe, Henry's brother, and his sister, Beth."

Grace took her seat between Beth and Big Jake. "There! Now you know everybody!" she giggled.

Sarah felt she needed to say something, so she stood up and said, "I want to let you all know what a pleasure it is to meet you and to thank you for inviting us." She sat down and looked at Henry. He smiled in such a way that let her know everything was all right.

"It's the least we could do," said Beth, looking at Sarah.

Hank spoke before Sarah had a chance to show that she felt there was an edge to Beth's comment. "Oh, good! Here come the waitresses! I'm starved!"

At that point, everyone started to mull over their menus. Sarah looked at Beth, who looked back with an odd look that was not particularly friendly.

25

Henry turned the Jeep off and carried Charlie into the cabin, car seat and all. He got the fire going again. This time it had gone completely out, but the cabin still was at 65 degrees.

Storm was so happy to see everybody return that Sarah allowed him into the cabin for a while. She changed Charlie and let him scoot in his walker for a while. "He didn't get much exercise today," she said aloud.

Henry laughed. "His mind did!"

"That's true, so did mine! You have a very kind family, Henry. You are very fortunate."

"They like you, Sarah. I can tell."

Sarah smiled. She was near tears, thinking of how she missed her mother.

"What's the matter?" Henry asked gently.

"I just miss her." A tear fell down Sarah's cheek and Henry brushed it away. He pulled her into his arms and held her tight. Sarah fought off the tears and took comfort in Henry's strong arms. He wasn't as tall as his father, but he was close. She loved how it felt when Henry held her. She loved how her ear came to his chest so she could hear his heart pound strong inside of him. She loved how he smelled. She loved how he made her feel safe. She loved Henry.

Charlie let out a giggly squeal. Henry's arms loosened and dropped down to Sarah's waist. "I think your little boy is getting a bath."

Sarah turned her head. Storm was licking Charlie's face.

"That's enough, Storm. He's clean."

Storm looked up and licked his nose. He walked over to the door and sat down. Henry looked down at Sarah and smiled. "I'm going to go start your car and let it run for a bit. I'll feed the chickens while I'm at it."

Sarah watched him through the window. She thought about this day they had spent together and wished it wouldn't end. At the same time, Henry was deep in his own thoughts. He thought of how Charlie didn't have a father, and all of the things that Sarah had been through on her own. How hard it was for her to be alone, without her mother, with no family other than Charlie. "And this Larry character," his thoughts continued, "if he ever comes near my Sarah, he will regret it."

"'My Sarah,'" Henry said aloud, "I like the sound of that." He was still yearning to tell Sarah that he loved her. His love grew more with each passing day. Still, he maintained control. He knew what sort of life he wanted. He wanted a wife and kids. And he wanted his kids to have the same rearing that he had growing up. He wanted a wife that held these same values, and though he did see much of that in Sarah, he had to be sure.

Henry was snapped out of his deep thoughts when Storm charged up to him wanting to play. He grabbed the stick out of the dog's mouth and threw it. He watched Storm chase after it and smiled to himself. Filling his arms up with firewood, he headed back to the cabin.

Sarah was in the rocking chair with Charlie. She turned and smiled at Henry as he closed the door and put the wood into the wood box.

"That is a sight a man can get used to," he thought to himself. He warmed his hands near the stove and told Sarah that he must be going. He had chores to do at home before dark.

Sarah's heart dropped a little, but knew all along that he'd be leaving. She stood up to put Charlie down in his crib. Henry tugged gently at her arm. "Let me see him first," he said.

Sarah turned the sleeping baby toward Henry, who smiled and kissed him on the forehead. "See you later, Sport."

Sarah tucked him in his crib. She walked back to Henry and looked into his eyes. "Thank you for a wonderful day, Henry. It truly was *wonderful*."

Her dark eyes sparkled with genuine happiness. He felt like blurting out, "I love you, Sarah!" But instead said," I'd really like you two to spend Christmas with my family and me. Please don't say no."

"I won't say 'no,' Henry. We'd love to join you."

There was an awkward pause between the two of them. Henry began to lean down toward Sarah. She stood still looking at him. "Is he going to kiss me?" she wondered. Her heart pounded as he drew nearer.

Henry wanted nothing more than to kiss her at that moment. But his mind raced, "Would it be too forward? Is it too soon?" He pulled Sarah as close to him as he could. She pressed her cheek against his strong chest and listened to his heart. They held each other for a moment then she felt Henry's hands on either side of her head as he made her face him. "I'll see you in three days," he said, then pressed his lips to her forehead and kissed her.

26

Three days. To Sarah, it sounded like an eternity. She decided to busy herself with making Christmas presents. Although at the commune they had not celebrated Christmas, her mother always found a way to get her a small gift to open. She told her the meaning of Christmas and of the Christmases of her childhood.

She embroidered a picture of pine cones and red ribbon on a flour sack towel for Grace. For Henry's father, she baked an assortment of cookies. She knitted a scarf for Henry, and for

Hank, she gave him a picture of Lake Serene in the summertime that she had sketched.

Sarah had to be creative when it came to wrapping the gifts. She wrapped them first in newspaper, then using the small amount of art supplies she had acquired through garage sales and auctions, she fancied them up. She set them on the dresser. "They actually look nice, Charlie, with the light flickering on them."

Charlie stared up at the colorful sparkles of the glitter. Sarah watched him. "Let's brighten our home up, too!" She cut out some stars from cardboard and decorated them with glue and glitter on both sides. Running a thread through a hole in one of the points, she tied it off then hung them in the windows. Charlie squealed with delight at the shiny objects and bounced up and down in his walker to the Christmas music on the radio.

Sarah laid out the clothes that they would be wearing for Christmas. She was glad that Henry had only invited them three days ago, if she had to wait much longer, it would have been hard to bear. She looked outside. It was snowing – a very pretty snow at that. Occasionally, Storm would run by in the path that led to the pump house, and then back down the path that led to the outhouse. His black fur barely collected any snow.

27

Sarah heard the blade of the plow coming up the driveway. Thanks to Henry and Hank, it was always kept clear. They also cleared a large area where she parked her car and broad paths to both the outhouse and to the pump house. Before he came in, Henry cleared the freshly fallen snow.

Her heart leapt with delight when she finally heard Henry knock on the door. Charlie's head turned to the knock. "Uh!" was all he could say.

Sarah smiled. "That's right, Honey; Henry is here."
She opened the door and Henry stepped in.

"Merry Christmas!"

"Merry Christmas to you! Would you like
some hot chocolate?"

"I'd love some," Henry said as he took his
coat off and hung it on a peg near the door. He sat
down at the table and looked around the room. "I
see you've been decorating! It looks nice."

"Charlie likes the sparkles," Sarah said as
she set a mug of hot chocolate down in front of
him. She cranked the radio and let the music play
softly in the background.

"You look nice, too."

Sarah blushed. "Thank you, Henry."

Charlie bounced in his walker, shaking his
jingle bells. Sarah had strung them together tightly
into a ring. It was easy for Charlie to grasp them
and he loved the noise they made.

Henry downed the last of his cocoa. "I'll
go start your car and let it warm up." He looked
around the cabin. "I see the wood box is full, as
well as the water jugs. Do you want me to feed the
chickens?"

"Already done," said Sarah. "I'll put some
long-burning logs on the fire and we'll be good to
go!"

It took about 10 minutes to get to Henry's parents' house from the church. They had a beautiful farmhouse with a large wrap-around porch. Though everything was covered in snow, Sarah could just imagine how nice it must look in the summertime, with the flowers and trees boasting their foliage.

Henry set the armload of Christmas presents down on the bench on the porch and held the door open for Sarah. Grace was just coming out of the kitchen to greet them, wiping her hands on her apron.

"Merry Christmas! Come in, come in! Oh, Sarah, let me hold Charlie while you take your coat off."

"Thank you, and Merry Christmas!"

Henry stepped in behind Sarah. "Here, I'll trade you," Sarah said to him, handing over her coat and taking the presents.

Henry hung the coats up in the closet near the door and placed their boots on the long narrow rug that lined a wall.

"It smells great in here, Mom! Merry Christmas!" He gave his mother a peck on the cheek.

"Come this way, you two," Grace said as she carried Charlie off to another room. Charlie started to cry as soon as Sarah was out of sight, though

215

it was only for a moment. Once she was beside Grace, he was fine.

"Look, Charlie," said Sarah, "a Christmas tree!"

Charlie stared at the bright lights while Sarah placed the very homemade-looking gifts under the tree. She stood up and looked at Grace. "Do you need help in the kitchen?"

Grace smiled, "Why, yes! I think I can use another hand. Thank you." She handed Charlie to Henry. "You boys can find something to amuse yourselves."

Charlie went readily to Henry. They were good buddies. Henry pointed out the different decorations around the house to Charlie, who cooed and babbled in amazement.

While Sarah helped in the kitchen, people continued to arrive. Grace would bustle out to greet everyone, and then come back to the kitchen. Clare and Jessica soon joined them and helped out while their husbands sat in the living room drinking their eggnog and visiting with Henry.

"Sarah and Jessica, if you could get all of the food into the serving dishes, I'll set them out on the table. Clare, will you go tell the guys that we'll be eating in about 10 minutes? Now, where is Beth?" Grace opened a door in the kitchen and called up the stairway, "Beth!"

In a few moments, Beth came down.

"Merry Christmas, Beth!" said Jessica.

"Merry Christmas!" Sarah also said.

"Merry Christmas, Aunt Jessica," was Beth's only reply.

"Beth, run out and tell Dad to get in here, please. We're about to eat," Grace said as she came into the kitchen from the dining room. Beth stepped into an enclosed porch off of the kitchen and put on a jacket and boots. Sarah continued to focus on the task in front of her.

When they were alone in the kitchen, Jessica said quietly, "Don't worry about her, Sarah, she's just moody."

While this did make Sarah feel a bit better, she couldn't help but feel that Beth's opinion of her wasn't related to her "moodiness."

It wasn't long before the door of the back porch opened and Beth and Big Jake stepped inside. They took their coats and boots off, then came into the kitchen. Big Jake washed his hands in the sink beside Sarah. "Hello, Sarah," he said in his low voice. "Merry Christmas! Merry Christmas, Jessica!"

"Merry Christmas!" the women chirped back in unison.

"Oh, good! You came right in! We're ready to eat right now," Grace said.

Big Jake bent down to kiss his wife. "It smells great, Honey."

As the crowd migrated from the living room to the dining room, Henry and Charlie came into the kitchen. Charlie eagerly reached for his mother. Sarah hugged and kissed him, as Henry guided her to her place at the table. They were seated at the large table while Little John, Jim, Paul, and Lisa sat at a smaller table off to the side.

The dinner was spectacular. A large beef roast, gravy, mashed potatoes, side dishes, and salads. The room was full of friendly voices and several childhood Christmas memories came out. It suddenly dawned on Sarah how fortunate she was to be living on Lake Serene with the opportunity to raise Charlie with such freedom. She shuddered when she thought of how he would have otherwise been raised. By the time he was three, her time with Charlie would have been limited, as he would be sent to "school." She could only imagine what they began to teach the boys at that young age. She recalled her school days. All of the children were homeschooled, so to speak. Not necessarily by his or her own parent. The boys and girls were separated for the most part, and while they were all taught the standard curriculum of the state, Larry's doctrine was also taught. "He has a chance, now," she thought to herself. There had been times when

Sarah wondered if what her mother was up to was right. After all, if she stayed at the commune, at least they'd still be together. But at what price? Any doubts that she had about her mother's decision had vanished then and there, at that Christmas dinner table. Sarah suddenly felt as though she were twice as strong, mentally and physically, as she had been when she awoke this morning. It felt invigorating.

28

While most had retired to the living room to stretch out and relax after dinner, Grace brought Sarah upstairs to the room Henry had as a boy. "You can change Charlie in here, and I set up this playpen for him to sleep in if he's tired."

"Thank you, Grace," said Sarah. Charlie was tired. Sarah had wanted to have him watch while people opened their gifts, but she knew it would be best for him to sleep. She changed him and laid him in the playpen. As she was covering him up, she felt a hand on her shoulder.

"That used to be my blanket," Henry said softly. "My Grandma knitted it for me. G'night, Buddy!"

Sarah and Henry joined the others in the living room. Grace was passing out gifts. Ribbons and paper were strewn about the floor. Grace tried to keep up with it, but finally surrendered. Sarah thanked Grace and Big Jake for the beautiful sweater they had given her and handed out her gifts to everyone.

"Oh, Sarah," Grace admired the towel. "This is just too pretty to use! You do very nice work!"

"And you can bake, too!" said Big Jake with a mouthful of cookie. He looked over at Hank. "What did you get, Dad?"

Hank lifted his head. He had a tear in his eye. He slowly turned the picture of Lake Serene around and held it up. Then turned it back toward himself and looked at it some more. The room grew quiet. Big Jake reached out to Grace's hand. John put his hand on Henry's shoulder. Sarah stood and watched Hank. She was confused. Had she done something wrong? Was she missing something?

Hank stood up, blew his nose and put his hanky into his back pocket. Looking Sarah in the eyes, he walked toward her. He gave her a hug and whispered, "It's the most beautiful, wonderful gift I have ever gotten in my whole life, Sarah. How did you know?"

Sarah hugged him back and closed her eyes in perplexed relief. "You're welcome, Hank. I love you," she whispered back.

"I love you, too, Sarah." Hank pulled away and sat back down in his chair. He looked at the picture some more, then gently wrapped the tissue back around it, and placed it back into the box. He was quite quiet for the rest of the day. Not sad, really, but just quiet.

29

It was dark when Henry steered the car up the driveway. Sarah was still wondering about the gift she had given Hank. Henry hadn't brought it up during the ride, so she didn't either. Their conversation was limited. Mostly, they listened to the radio.

Henry backed the car up to the porch. "You stay right here for a minute, I'll grab a lantern."

Sarah reached over the seat of the car and released the harness that held Charlie. "Come here, Pumpkin," she said softly. "We're home."

Henry came out with the lantern and Storm wagged his tail eagerly as he followed him out of the porch. He opened the car door, holding the light so Sarah could easily see her way to the cabin.

"It's pretty cold in here. Keep him wrapped up," Henry instructed. "I'll get the fire going."

Sarah sat in the rocker with Charlie on her lap and watched Henry. She couldn't take it any longer. She had to ask him what it was about the gift she had given Hank. "Henry," she said softly, as Henry struck a match on the cast iron surface, "why was there such a significant reaction to the present that I gave to Hank?"

Henry stood with his back to her holding the burning match, then dropped it quickly into the firebox when it nearly burned his fingers. He struck another and lit the paper beneath the kindling. Slowly turning around, he knelt down beside her. "You mean you don't know?" he looked at Sarah with astonishment. Sarah's eyes raced his face, shifting back and forth, up and down, as she tried to read his thoughts.

"Know what?"

"You don't know, do you? I mean, how could you, unless Grandpa told you. And he wouldn't do that. He never talks about it..." Henry was now pacing the floor.

"Henry," Sarah nearly demanded, "what are you talking about?"

"Have you ever been in Grandpa's house?"

"No, I haven't. Why?"

He paced some more, completely baffled.

"Henry," Sarah softened her tone, "please tell me what is going on."

Henry pulled out a chair from the table and sat down in front of the stove, facing Sarah. "My Grandma, Grandma Jacobson, passed away years ago. It was hard on Grandpa. It was so sudden and unexpected. They used to come here, to Lake Serene, all the time in the summer. Grandpa would keep an eye on the place when your family wasn't using it. One day while Grandpa was out fishing, Grandma came along, as she often did, to sketch. She was an artist, a very good artist." Henry paused for a moment, and then continued. "On this particular day, Grandpa was returning in the canoe. He saw Grandma lying on the hill beside her easel. He called, but she didn't move. He paddled as fast as he could, then jumped out of the canoe as soon as he hit shallow water. He ran to her, calling her name, but there was no response. He carried her to the truck and rushed her to the hospital. But he knew it was too late."

"I'm so sorry, Henry." Sarah's eyes were welling up with tears.

Henry put his hand up. "Let me finish. We laid her to rest and Grandpa never came back here. He just couldn't bring himself to do it. When Grandpa told us that he had fished Lake Serene again, we couldn't believe what were hearing, and he actually seemed rejuvenated somehow. It was so neat to see him as his old self again. We didn't understand the change, and of course we wondered who this 'Sarah' was that he kept talking about... Mom insists the angels sent you..." Henry smiled and looked at Sarah then continued. "Anyway, after the funeral, Dad came over here and made sure everything was locked up and put away. He gathered up all of Grandma's art things, including her last sketch that was only half finished." Then he looked deep into Sarah's eyes. "Sarah, the sketch that you gave Grandpa was the same scene that Grandma had been working on when she died. It's nearly identical."

Sarah looked at Henry. She didn't know how to react. To her, the view that she sketched was just simply picturesque. She hadn't really put any deep thought into why she chose to sketch it, she just did. She gave it to Hank because she knew he loved Lake Serene. He had always been the happy, good-natured man she met that day at Carson's Spring. If his personality had been otherwise, she guessed she didn't care to know about it.

Henry was still looking at Sarah. He looked as though he was expecting some sort of explanation.

"Henry, I'm flattered that your mother thinks the angels sent me, but I think this is all coincidence. You know, like artists of the same taste. We were in the same place. Other than the cabin, really, the only thing to sketch here is the lake."

"Yes, I know. It's just that they are both so much alike. It's as though you both stood in the same spot and took the same snapshot." Henry smiled lightly. "At any rate, that is why we all reacted the way we did. Sarah, you've lifted Grandpa's spirits immensely and we all appreciate that. We are fortunate to have you as a part of our lives."

"The feeling is mutual, Henry," Sarah replied. "I don't know if I would have been able to stay here if I hadn't met your grandpa. If anything, I would say the angels sent *him* to *me*."

30

The cold Minnesota winter began to give way to spring. It was mid-March and the days were longer and warmer. The snow was melting. The chickens loved to get out of their cage and scratch around in the areas that had been kept clear of deep snow. All of the hens had made it, except one. She was old and, perhaps, her time was due.

Most days were warm enough where Sarah could leave the cabin door open and let the heat of the woodstove flow out into the enclosed porch.

She took great advantage of this and used it as a sort of greenhouse to start many of her vegetables for her garden. She had made sure to save enough seeds from last year to plant her garden this year. She even had potatoes left over to use as seed potatoes. However, it was uncomfortably close. She preferred to have enough potatoes to eat until at least mid-summer *and* have some for seed potatoes. Plus, since Charlie would be eating more by next winter, she knew that she would need to increase her yield.

Hank had given her a seed catalog that specialized in heritage seeds, which meant the seeds could all be saved for the following year's crop. Until now, Sarah had thought that all seeds possessed this ability. Hank told her about hybrids and of how their seeds may or may not reproduce. Or if they do, they may not produce quality fruits. Sarah could not waste her time and effort on such a chance.

Charlie was beginning to walk almost stumble-free. He was well aware of the hot stove and never went near enough to burn himself. He loved walking around the cabin like a big boy! Sarah kept a small box of toys for him near the dresser. He would entertain himself with them, but now that the porch was open during the day, he barely paid them any mind.

Today Sarah was in the rocker on the porch, plotting out her garden and carefully reviewing the catalog for seeds that she wanted to order. She set a $25 limit on herself, satisfied that amount would get her a large variety of fruits and vegetables. One type of seed she was particularly looking forward to was popcorn!

Charlie was playing with a ball, throwing it the best he could, and then retrieving it. He stopped when Storm started to bark. Sarah could hear the tractor approaching. It was quite large and branches on either side of the driveway brushed against the cab. She was expecting Henry to come by one of these days. He was going to clear her garden area somewhat to expose the ground. Once thawed, he'd bring Suzie and Elaine over to plow it up. He could just use his tractor to plow, but he liked to work the horses and keep them well trained. They were a hobby of Henry's.

The chickens scattered as the tractor moved about the area, then quickly regrouped to the freshly exposed earth to peck at any new findings. When he had finished, he parked the tractor and climbed down out of the cab.

Sarah and Henry had been growing closer and closer in the past months. Henry had taken Sarah and Charlie out to lunch a few times and Grace had invited them to an occasional Sunday dinner. Sarah felt very comfortable with his family; even Beth was warming up to her. Sarah thought what really charmed her was Charlie. For some reason, he was drawn to Beth. Henry once commented on how Charlie made Beth smile more than anybody he knows.

Henry stepped into the porch and scooped up Charlie as he waddled his way toward him. "Hey, Buddy-boy!" Henry kissed his cheek. "Hi, Sarah."

"Hi, Henry. How was it driving the tractor over here?"

"Not bad! Actually, it was kind of a fun ride! I was thinking maybe you and Charlie might like to ride back with me, and I'll bring you home in the pickup."

"That sounds like fun! What do you think, Charlie?"

31

Charlie was in awe when sitting way up high in the tractor cab. His eyes were wide as he looked around. He'd point and say things like, "Dah-doo!" Which, Sarah was confident, made perfect sense to him.

The tractor rolled down dirt roads through the countryside and meandered its way back to Henry's place. He lived in a small house that was on Hank's land. He worked along with his grandpa and dad on both of their farms. Hank raised crops and his dad raised beef cattle and pigs. Sarah liked to visit the farms, but even with all of the modern amenities, she still preferred her little log cabin on Lake Serene.

Henry used to be concerned about her living without the things he had always taken for granted, but this concern waned as he became accustomed to dealing without electricity and indoor plumbing whenever he was at her place.

On the way back to Lake Serene, Henry took a detour down a narrow road. Until recently, the snow had kept him from venturing down it. This road was private and was not maintained by the county.

"Where are we going?" Sarah asked, tightening her grip on Charlie as the pickup rolled slowly forward, rocking back and forth.

"I just want to show you something." Henry had a boyish grin on his face. Sarah smiled and looked out into the thickness of the pine trees on either side of the truck. They drove nearly a half a mile into the trees when they came to a clearing. Now on either side of them were two fields. In one field, a herd of deer perked their heads up and focused their large ears toward the noise. They were far enough away that they didn't sense an immediate threat from the truck that was slowly rolling through their territory.

The fields ended and they again were on a narrow road through the trees. However, they were not quite as thick as the pines. And while there were a lot of pines, there were also maples, oaks, and birch. Another clearing came. Henry stopped the truck. To the left there was a barn and a few smaller buildings. In front of them was a large log house. Though it was in need of some repair, Sarah could imagine how beautiful it once was. It had a wide stairway that led to a great porch. The house itself was perhaps five times the size of her cabin, plus it had an upper level with dormer windows. There were three chimneys, she observed.

"What is this, Henry?" she asked, still staring at the house.

"This is what was always referred to as 'The Lodge.' Come on, I'll show you." Henry got out of the truck.

"It doesn't look very safe to go in," Sarah said stepping out her door.

"Oh, we won't go inside – there is something else." Henry took her hand and led her to the back of the house. Behind the house was a large cleared area, which Sarah guessed would be a yard. At the very end of the yard, the ground sloped down toward a lake, still covered with questionable ice. They walked to the edge of the shore. "Wow, this makes Lake Serene look puny!" Sarah said.

Henry pointed across the lake to where the trees gave way to a channel. "Do you see there? Where that channel is?" He had one arm around Sarah and brought his cheek close to hers so he could line her up to look in the right direction. "That will lead you right into Lake Serene."

Sarah hadn't really explored Lake Serene. Her first year had been so busy getting accustomed to her new life, and it wasn't something she could do with Charlie yet. Besides, Hank and Henry provided her with all the fish she could eat. Sometimes she fished off shore, but for the most part, the men shared their bounty with her.

"It's beautiful, and I'm sure even more so in the summertime." Her mind was now drifting away from the scenic view and to the warm feeling she got whenever Henry touched her.

"Oh, it is," said Henry, now standing tall again. He looked at down at Sarah then wrapped both her and Charlie in his strong arms. "Beautiful. Just like you two." He pulled them in close to his chest. Sarah could hear his heart pound hard, even through the thickness of his chore jacket.

Henry showed Sarah around the grounds of The Lodge. He described the inside of the house the best he could, as the windows were boarded up. He did have the key to the door and thought it was okay to go in, but didn't say anything because he knew Sarah would be uncomfortable bringing Charlie inside, given the state of the roof.

Sarah admired the old log buildings. They held as much charm and warmth to her as her own little log home. "Whose place is this, Henry?" she asked.

"It belongs to you! This is the house that your great-grandfather built when he got married. They had a bunch of kids – you'd have to ask Grandpa about all of that. He knew all of your relatives."

Sarah's mind was in a dream. She envisioned children laughing and running around, up and down the porch step, slamming the screen door. Their father would be working out in the fields with the older boys, if there were any, perhaps they were all girls. The inside of The Lodge was beautiful with its grand fireplace and open stairway going up to the second level. Their mother would be in the kitchen, getting ready to feed her brood.

Sarah brought herself back to the present time. "Henry, can we go now? There is something I'd like to do, and I'll need your help, if you don't mind."

"Sure," said Henry, not asking any questions. After all, he was certain to find out what Sarah was up to soon enough.

32

Sarah pulled hard on one handle of the heavy trunk while Henry pushed it awkwardly up the log rail ladder from the root cellar. "Personal family stuff," Sarah thought. That's how Hank had put it. Sarah guessed it was time to learn more about herself and her family.

Henry closed the cellar door and stood near the stove for a moment to warm his hands. It was still quite cool in the root cellar. Sarah moved the table and chairs back into place, then knelt in front of the trunk and opened it slowly. What she was expecting was photographs, for the most part, but she really wasn't certain of what she would find.

The contents were covered with a single bed sheet. Underneath were framed photographs and books, all individually wrapped in paper. Sarah opened them one by one and set them on the table. Even though it was still light outside, Henry needed an oil lamp to read the backs of the pictures. They were old sepia and black and white photos taken long ago. The faces were new to Sarah, but the buildings were easily recognized.

While Henry read the names and dates, if any were given, Sarah continued to unpack the trunk. She came across a leather-bound book. Opening it randomly to the middle, she read aloud,

"'April 1886 - Severe tornado tore through Sauk Rapids. They say over 50 people died. Many more injured. We were fortunate not to have experienced tragic weather this far north. Many of us men are loading up the buckboards and wagons with what supplies we can spare and heading down to the area to help before we need to return for spring planting.'"

She closed the journal and set it aside. "I'll be reading this, to be sure!" she said.

One of the last things she pulled out of the trunk was a rather large box. It was tied shut with string. She stood up, set it on the table and carefully untied it. Lifting the lid she saw the contents were packed quite tightly with tissue paper. Sarah unpacked it as gently as it had obviously been packed. "Will you look at this!" she exclaimed eagerly, pulling out a large ceramic cookie jar. It was in the shape of a fat, happy pig. "This should be on display to enjoy, not tucked away in an old trunk."

"Is it empty?" Henry teased, rubbing his stomach.

"I'm afraid so! But you're welcome to stay for supper."

"I'd love to. I'll get the chores done while you cook." Henry stood and put on his jacket. On the way out the door, he grabbed the empty water jugs, which were threaded together by a length of rope, hanging from one of the pegs in the log wall.

33

Charlie had just woken from his nap as Sarah finished dishing up supper. Henry loved to help Charlie eat. "He is getting so big. Huge, compared to when I met him last July," Henry observed.

"Yes, he is," Sarah agreed. "You know, part of me wants him to just stay a baby, and not grow up...but at the same time it is so fun to see him change and grow."

It was a bit earlier than when Sarah and Charlie usually ate, but Sarah knew that Henry would have to be leaving soon to get his evening chores done, and she didn't want that to be the reason why he couldn't stay for supper.

"That was delicious, Sarah. Thank you." Henry was relaxing in the rocking chair near the stove.

"You're welcome. Next time I'll make sure the pig is full of cookies for dessert," Sarah said as she cleaned up Charlie and set him next to his toy box. He reached in and grabbed a toy from inside. Sarah knelt on the floor and demonstrated the movable parts of the toy, encouraging fascination on Charlie's part. She smiled and praised him when he would gleefully clap his hands as he mastered a new skill.

Henry watched the two of them from the rocker, thinking how naturally being a mother seemed to come to Sarah, and how determined she was to give Charlie the best that life had to offer. And here, in this next-to-bare little cabin out in the woods, Henry felt he was watching two of the happiest people on earth. To Henry, Sarah was the most beautiful woman he had ever laid eyes upon. He was deeply in love with her.

When Sarah stood up, Charlie hadn't even noticed. He continued to play with his toys. Sarah walked back toward the stove and noticed Henry looking at her.

"Penny for your thoughts," she said softly.

Henry stood up, still looking at her. He picked up both of her hands, held them in his and said, "Sarah, I love you." He leaned down and kissed her gently on the lips, then pulled back, looking at her as though to see if what he had done was all right.

He could see by the way her brown eyes shined, that it was perfectly all right.

"I love you, too, Henry Jacobson."

The afternoon was late when he left Sarah's, but Henry still drove home slowly. He needed to be alone with his thoughts for a while before joining the other guys in doing chores. He drove down the long driveway and parked in front of The Lodge. He didn't get out of the truck, but just sat and thought. He sat and thought for nearly a half an hour.

"I'm going to fix this place up and surprise Sarah," he said aloud. He put the truck in gear, and headed home.

34

The sun was just barely coming over the lake when Sarah woke up. She routinely added wood to the fire and made herself a cup of tea. Soon she would no longer need to heat the cabin all night. It was late in April and the nights were growing quite mild. In fact, if it were only for her, there would be some nights where she wouldn't bother with a fire. But Charlie kicked his blankets off all night long, and it would be too cold for him.

Sarah stood at the window overlooking the lake and watched the sun rise. It was a sight of which she never tired. Charlie stirred in his crib. She looked over at him and smiled. He recently had his first birthday. How quickly the time passed amazed Sarah. He was walking around with more confidence and starting to talk a lot more. Her baby was becoming a little boy.

Today she made a trip to town. There was laundry to be done, and dog food to buy. As she drove through Lone Pine, she spotted Henry. She hadn't seen him for a couple of weeks. He was busy, she reasoned, with all the calves being born, plus the additional chores that came with springtime.

He was carrying a bag out of the hardware store. Sarah was about to honk lightly on the horn to get his attention when the pretty blonde from the Fourth of July booth came trotting after him from inside the hardware store. She looped one arm through Henry's and was smiling and twisting one of her bouncy curls around a finger on her other hand.

Sarah didn't honk, but instead continued her drive to the Laundromat with a pang of jealousy.

Had she been privy to the conversation between Henry and Miss Bouncy Curls, however, she would have quickly learned that her jealous feelings were unwarranted.

"Henry!" said the syrupy voice. "Daddy says your stove pipe will be in next Monday."

"Thank you, Darla. I'll pick it up then," Henry replied politely, still walking forward.

Darla Taylor had been after Henry's attention since she began to notice boys. Henry, on the other hand, had no interest in her. He found her to be conceited, too forward, and dim-witted. He had held this opinion of her since the first grade.

"I'll be working that Saturday," Darla pressed on, "I'll help you with your order, if you like."

"Whoever is available to help will be fine; don't put yourself out," Henry said, still trying to be polite. He stopped and set the bag in the back of his pickup, then opened the cab door.

"Henry Jacobson, don't you even recognize when a girl is trying to get your attention?" Darla said in a melodramatic scold.

Henry stopped and looked directly at Darla. "Darla, somebody already has my attention, and it isn't you."

"Well!" she huffed with her hands on her hips. "Do you mean that Plain Jane that lives in a hut out in the woods? What in the world does she have that I don't have?"

"She has class, for one thing, and a whole lot more. Good day, Darla." Henry tipped his hat and climbed into his truck.

Darla Taylor spun on her heels with her arms crossed in front of her and stomped back to her daddy's hardware store, her blonde curls swinging and bouncing with fury.

35

As the day wore on, Sarah had re-evaluated her initial reaction to what she saw in front of the hardware store. "Henry would never see anything in a girl like that," her thoughts reasoned. "And besides, he said he loved me. I believe he meant that."

She unloaded the car then prepared lunch. Charlie normally took just one nap per day now, right after lunch. He usually slept from about noon until three. These three hours were valuable to Sarah, as she was able to get a lot of work done.

Her porch was full of plants that would prove to be more than ready for transplanting into the garden in a few weeks. She was excited because one of her hens was setting on a clutch. She expected to see baby chicks in about 19 days! But the most exciting thing of all would be the goat that Hank was bringing her at any moment. It was an older Nubian milk goat that was due to kid at any time. Hank got it for free at an auction. Nobody wanted her. She was too old, and most feared she was too weak to kid, or would produce less milk than was worth the bother.

To her surprise, and her joy, it was Henry's truck and trailer that pulled up into the driveway. She could hear the echoing "Naahaha!" of the goat in the large horse trailer.

Hank stepped out into the somewhat-muddy driveway. "She's here, Sarah!" he smiled and headed to the back of the trailer.

Henry walked toward Sarah and gave her a hug and a kiss. "Boy, I've missed you," he said.

Sarah smiled and put her hand in his. "It has been awhile, hasn't it?" Her thoughts were sharply interrupted when Storm came running up from the lake, barking wildly at the strange new noise. "Storm! No!" Sarah yelled. The dog mellowed, but still barked. Henry opened a compartment on the side of the trailer and pulled out a long horse lead.

He grabbed Storm's collar and snapped the lead onto the ring under the dog's jaw, then pulled him toward the edge of the woods and tied him to a tree. Storm continued to bark for a while, then finally just sat and watched.

Hank brought the goat out on another lead. It too, had a collar around its neck. "Naahaha!" it said as it held its head high and looked at the new surroundings.

Hank handed the lead to Sarah. "Here you go! We have some panels to make a temporary pen for her. And we'll put up a little shelter, too."

The men went to work. Sarah pet the goat and led her gently around. Her body was huge and it was obvious that she would be having her babies any day. She so wanted to wake Charlie, but he had only been sleeping for half an hour. The goat nibbled on grass that had been buried underneath snow all winter. She seemed to be sampling what her new home had to offer.

Hank and Henry were assembling four walls of a small shelter on a flat hill near the chicken pen. The walls were already put together individually, so all they had to do was attach them at the corners. Three of them were equal in size, five feet long by five feet tall. These made up the north, east, and west walls. The fourth was only three feet long by five feet tall. This one had the warm southern exposure and would allow the goat into the shelter through the two-foot doorway.

Once the walls were assembled, they attached a truss for the roof that created an angle so the rain would shed off the back end of the structure. With the shed complete, and lined with a plush layer of straw, the men then put up a portable corral. It consisted of several panels of heavy woven steel that were connected together. All they had to do was unfold it and arrange it to make a large circle around the shed. Its overall size would be quite large, as each panel was eight feet long. They pounded steel posts into the ground and secured the panels to them. The last thing was the gate that provided easy access in and out of the pen.

"Let's put her in there!" said Henry.

Sarah led the goat through the gate and into the pen. Being such an old goat, she followed along easily. Hank followed them in with a shallow rubber tub. "Henry, go fetch some water," he instructed, then went back to the trailer.

Sarah still had the goat on the lead. She showed her the inside of the shed, and then led her around the fenced area.

As Henry returned with the water, Hank returned with an armful of alfalfa hay.

"Go ahead and unhook her, Sarah. She's not going anywhere now!"

Sarah unfastened the lead from the goat's collar. The goat walked to the water and took a drink, then nibbled on the hay. She acted as though she'd lived there her whole life.

"Yep. It won't be long now. I think we're lucky we got her here today," Hank observed. Henry came into the pen with Storm still on his leash. "Henry, git that dog outta here!"

"I will, Grandpa, if he acts up. He has to get his curiosity out of him," Henry said. He led Storm closer to the goat. The goat didn't seem fearful, but that was likely because Storm wasn't barking. Henry carefully let the dog sniff at the goat, the barn, and the water bucket. Soon he lost interest and just sat down.

"It's almost time to get Charlie up. I want to show him our new critter!" Sarah said. She walked out through the gate, followed by the two men and the dog.

36

While Sarah changed Charlie, Hank shared his knowledge of goat-raising with her. "An' you'll have to milk her twice a day, no ifs, ands, or buts…"

Sarah listened while Henry observed Storm from a window inside the cabin. The dog seemed to be content with the new addition. He was just lying near the pen, watching the goat.

"You're going to have two more goats within a day or two, Sarah," Henry said. "She's ready." He joined Hank at the kitchen table. "In a matter of weeks you'll wonder why you bothered with buying milk at all!"

"An' butter, an' cheese," chimed Hank.

"It's all just so exciting! Let's show Charlie the goat!" Sarah said, heading out the door.

Charlie couldn't take his eyes off the new addition to their yard. He pointed and grunted one syllable "words." Henry picked up a large stump that had not been split and threw it into the pen, then went inside the pen to position it near the center.

"What's that for?" Sarah asked.

"For the kids to climb on. It's simple, but they'll love it."

"We best get goin', Henry. Keep a close eye on her, Sarah," said Hank, walking to the truck.

Henry put his arm around Sarah. "I'll come by early in the morning to see how she's doing. It may still be dark, so don't be alarmed." He bent down and scooped up Charlie. "See you tomorrow, Buddy!"

Hank was watching them from the cab. "Now that is a nice view," he thought to himself, seeing Henry walking with one arm around Sarah, and Charlie held high up in his other arm.

37

It was barely five o'clock a.m. when Henry returned to Sarah's. As he pulled into the driveway, he saw a lantern out on the stump in the goat pen and Sarah kneeling beside it. He jogged over to the pen and let himself in through the gate. "Did she have them?"

"Yes," said Sarah softly. "Three of them! About an hour ago."

Henry looked in the small shelter. Two of the kids were lying down and one was taking advantage of having its mother all to itself. The

261

mother stood chewing its cud and looked back at Henry.

"Did all three get to drink?" he asked.

"Yes, a couple of times. They look perfectly healthy."

"How long have you been out here?"

"About two hours, I couldn't sleep. I found myself getting up, looking out the window, pacing the floor, then lying down again for a little bit of a snooze. Finally, the last time I got up, I heard her so I came out right when the third one was born."

The sky was starting to turn orange as the sun made its morning appearance.

"Come inside, Henry. I'll make some breakfast for you." Sarah pulled on his hand.

Henry grabbed the lantern and walked toward the cabin with her. He turned the lantern out when they reached the porch. "Wait, Sarah. Let's watch the sun come up."

The young couple stood at the edge of the hill that overlooked Lake Serene. It was a beautiful sight. Sarah rubbed off the chill of the morning air from her shoulders. Henry pulled her in front of him and wrapped his arms around her to keep her warm. They didn't speak. They just both faced the lake and watched the dawn of a new day.

Henry thought of the work he had been secretly doing at The Lodge. It was true that he was busy working the farms, but every spare moment away from his regular workday was spent working on The Lodge. He was nearly finished with the roof, except for the shingles. The next phase would be to repair any damage to the second floor. It was minimal for the most part. Mainly, it needed a good cleaning. Some of the furniture needed repair and the bed mattresses had to be replaced. Henry already hauled away the old ones.

Downstairs everything was in pretty good shape. It was dusty, but in good shape. The grand woodstove had a bit of surface rust, but was readily removed with the regular use it was now receiving. One of the first things Henry did was clean all of the stovepipes and chimney flues. He then would use a different stove or the fireplace while he worked just to make sure they were all in proper working order.

He also got all of the pumps working. There was one in the kitchen with a sink that drained into a five-gallon bucket beneath it. Another was just outside the house, and a third one was out near the barns.

"I never get tired of this," Sarah interrupted his thoughts. The sun was now a huge orange globe, just above the tree line on the far end of the lake. A lane of its reflection formed all the way across the glassy surface of the freshly thawed water.

"It is a view," Henry commented while deciding at the same time tomorrow he would check out the sunrise at The Lodge.

38

Sarah's days were consumed with work. After two weeks, she began to take Old Mama, which she now called the mother goat, out of the pen and tied her up on the hillside behind the cabin. The vegetation there was all alfalfa, for the most part. At first the kids and Old Mama called and called to each other, but eventually became accustomed to the routine. Sarah would milk out what the kids didn't drink, which wasn't much, then milked her out in the evening before returning her to the pen for the night. The evening milking gave her nearly a gallon of milk. She used this milk to bottle feed the kids throughout the day.

In a few weeks, they'd be separated from each other completely and receive only the milk that Sarah gave them from the bottle. She had two does and one billy. The billy would be brought to the auction and sold. The does she'd keep for breeding. Old Mama would be milked, and then just be allowed to retire.

The mother hen now had 14 chicks peeping around her. Charlie loved to watch them, and Storm had given up pestering the chickens. He now had more interest in the goats.

Hank and Henry had put up a small pasture with a shelter for the goats in the alfalfa field. It was constructed of T-posts and woven wire. This enabled Sarah to keep the kids separate from Old Mama all night.

Henry had come with Suzie and Elaine and plowed Sarah's garden area. It was so much easier to work this year as the broken soil went much deeper than what she had dug up by hand last year. All of the cooler weather crops, such as potatoes, onions, carrots, and peas were in the ground. Today she was putting in corn and beans. She used the plastic that was carefully removed from the chicken pen to cover the rows at night in order to keep the soil warm and protect from any potential frost.

This year she was also planting beans and peas that could be stored dry to use for soups and chili. She was glad that these would only need to be shelled and not canned. This was something she could do inside the cabin on rainy days, or even into the winter, when there was plenty of time in her day.

While Sarah was busy in her garden, Henry was still busy at The Lodge. He finally had all of the windows cleaned, inside and out. The roof was completed. The wood floors had been swept and wiped down with a damp mop. He even washed all of the dishes and kitchen utensils. The place was nearly ready to be moved into, except for one thing: he hadn't told Sarah yet. He hadn't told anybody. He was still far from ready, as there were repairs to the barns and fences to be made.

He sat on the porch and pulled a sandwich from his cooler, thinking of where he'd start on the barn. He always liked this barn. It also was constructed from logs, and the inside was neat. As a boy, Henry remembered being inside. It had large box stalls for horses on one side and feed stalls on the other, with a broad walkway down the center. In one corner was a storage room and in another was where the feed was kept. A log ladder led to the hay loft above, which Henry had only been allowed to go up a couple of times.

There were fruit trees in the front yard –
plum, apple, and pear. Their leaves were noticeably
larger every time Henry pulled in the driveway.
He had plowed up the garden area with Suzie and
Elaine the same day he plowed Sarah's garden
at the cabin. This was quite a bit harder to do, as
the ground hadn't been broken up in years. This
garden had a nice woven fence all the way around
it. A deer could leap in, but with a dog outside all
night, it would easily be scared off.

"Perhaps I'm getting ahead of myself,"
Henry thought. He finished his second sandwich,
drank several cups of cold water from the pump,
and went back to work.

39

66 Naahaha!" the little billy goat cried
as Sarah put him in the chicken cage.
It was just barely large enough for him. Today he
was going to be sold at the auction. She set the
cage on a thick quilt in the back seat of the car.
Charlie giggled at his company! She put Charlie's
wagon in the trunk and they set off to the auction
barn. There were a lot of people there today. Sarah
guessed this was the busiest she had ever seen it.
With Charlie riding in the wagon along with the
goat in the cage, Sarah pulled the two of them

toward a trailer that was set up in the parking lot near the auction house. She was able to register to sell the goat there, instead of going inside. A man put a rope around the billy's neck, picked him up and took him away. That was the last Sarah and Charlie saw of him.

There was about a half an hour before the auction was to start, so Sarah decided to see what was to be auctioned off outside. She brought the empty cage back to her car and pulled Charlie around in the wagon.

There were a lot of ducks, geese, and chickens, many which were accompanied by offspring. Sarah put a kitten in Charlie's lap – a woman had a box of them that read "FREE" on it. She considered it, but handed the kitten back to the woman. The woman smiled and called, "Come back if you change your mind!" as Sarah pulled the wagon away.

She was scanning the lots for canning jars when she nearly ran into somebody.

"Oh! Excuse me!"

"No harm done," said the stranger, not moving. Sarah tried to maneuver her wagon around him, but he stepped to block her. "Say, aren't you that Sarah girl that lives *all* alone out in the woods?"

Sarah looked up at him. He had a toothpick sticking out of one corner of his crudely smiling mouth.

"Please let us by," Sarah said.

"Aren't you scared to be out there by yourself?" he continued, putting a dirty hand on her shoulder. "You should have someone to protect you."

Sarah brushed his hand off and fought back any signs of fear and the tears that she could feel building up inside of her.

"Please let us by," she said sternly, looking directly into his eyes.

He stepped closer to Sarah, "What's the rush? The auction doesn't start for 15 minutes…" He was interrupted by a giant hand clapping down on his shoulder. He cowered when he heard the low voice behind him.

"The calves are selling in the barn, Robert, not out here. There isn't anything for you out here."

"I…I…I was just trying to be neighborly, Big Jake, that's all," Bob stammered, trying to smile at the man.

Big Jake's face had no signs of amusement. "The calves are selling in the barn," Big Jake repeated.

Bob McCarthy trotted away like a dog with its tail between its legs.

Sarah let out a breath of relief. She looked up at Big Jake. She didn't know what to say, but he immediately made the situation less awkward. "Good morning, Sarah." He tipped his hat. "Lots of people here, aren't there?"

"Yes," was all she could say.

Charlie squealed and Sarah was relieved as Big Jake crouched down to shake his hand. "Hi, Charlie," he seemed to make his voice as gentle as he could. And even though he was crouching, Charlie still had to tilt his head way back to see Big Jake's face. "Are you having a good time, Buddy?" He patted Charlie's head, which looked small compared to the man's hand.

Big Jake stood up and turned to Sarah. "Enjoy your day," he softly smiled.

"Thank you, you too," she replied.

They looked at each other briefly knowing nothing more needed to be said. She watched as nearly everyone he passed greeted him. He was a well-respected man in these parts. Sarah couldn't help but to feel proud to know him and thankful to have an example of a man like him for Charlie.

40

Summertime approached quickly for Henry. It was early on a Saturday in June and he had the day off. The Jacobson men rotated the weekends so that they all would get a couple of weekends off each month. This morning he was down by the lake at The Lodge. He was watching the sun rise from the bench that he built and positioned specifically for this purpose. Henry knew that through the channel across the lake, Sarah was watching the sun rise over Lake Serene.

He longed for the day when they would watch every sunrise together.

He was deep in thought as the morning slowly brightened. His work here was done and he was contemplating his next move. A familiar sound came from up near The Lodge. He heard the truck door slam shut. Henry didn't bother to move. He knew his father would come down to the lake and sit with him.

For a while, the men said nothing to each other. They just took in the sights and sounds that accompanied a still lake in northern Minnesota – the calm waves lapping at the shore, an occasional call of a loon, the splash of a muskrat. It was a favorite time of day for many that lived in these parts.

Finally, the silence was broken. "I'm going to ask her to marry me, Dad."

"I know that, Son," his father answered.

The men sat in silence for another moment. "What if she says no?" Henry asked.

"She won't." Henry's father exuded more confidence than any man he knew. Henry strived to have that confidence himself, but part of him felt there was a chance that Sarah could decide that marrying Henry Jacobson was not in her plans.

His father continued, "You did a fine job on The Lodge. She'll love it."

"Thanks. I think this is the closest to the twentith century that I'll get her, but it's plush compared to the cabin."

"You'll be independent and your own man out here. There is nothing wrong with that. It will make you strong. Not just physically, but mentally, as well."

The two men continued to sit as the sun rose higher above the tree line. Big Jake thought to himself how the talk he had planned to give Henry about marriage wasn't going to be necessary after all. Both Sarah and Henry had the same values. This wasn't puppy love; they were really in love. They were both mature enough at their young ages of 20 and 25 to know the responsibilities that lay ahead of them, especially where Charlie was concerned. He then turned his thoughts to Grace. "Your mother is going to be pleased as punch," Big Jake said. "When are you going to propose?"

Henry smiled. "Soon."

41

Sarah was working in the garden when Henry's truck pulled up. She stood up straight and brushed a few wisps of hair out of her eyes with a soiled garden glove. Smiling, she walked carefully down the row of beans to greet him.

Henry watched her. "Just look at you," he thought to himself. "Even covered in dirt, you're the most beautiful woman in the world." He climbed out of the truck and walked toward her.

The smiles on both of their faces grew broader the closer they got to each other.

Sarah squinted as the sun shined in her eyes so Henry took his straw hat off and put it on her head. He gave her a hug and a kiss. "You look good in my hat," he said, "even though it is a bit large."

Sarah giggled. "What are you up to this fine day?"

"I have to go help set up for the Fourth of July festival and I thought I'd stop by to say hello. I also wanted to see if you and Charlie would want to join me at the festival the entire day of the Fourth."

"We'd…" Sarah started.

Henry put his hand up, "Wait until you hear me out. It's not as simple as you may think. I'd be picking you up very early in the morning, before sunrise."

"Oh," Sarah said. "Hmmm…it could be a long day for Charlie, but an exciting one! You can't talk us out of it. There is one catch, though."

"What's that?"

"This year, you bring *both* of us on the Ferris wheel."

Henry smiled, "You have a deal. I'll pick you up early on the Fourth. That's only four days away, so don't forget."

"I won't, Henry."

Henry looked at Sarah just for the sake of looking at her. He hugged her again and said, "I love you, Sarah."

"I love you, too."

"I don't want to, but I have to get on with my day. If I get a chance, I'll stop by before the fourth. Otherwise, I'll see you in a few days." Henry trotted back to his truck, started it up and drove down the driveway.

Sarah watched as the truck disappeared through the trees. She was heading to the cabin to check on Charlie when she realized that she still had Henry's hat on her head. A big grin came across her face, "Oh, you'll be back before the Fourth. I bet you'll be back today!" she said out loud.

42

Henry did come back later that day, and each morning up until the Fourth. His day just didn't seem to start right without seeing Sarah first.

Just as he said, it was very early when Henry came by to pick them up. But Sarah was prepared. She had all of her chores done. Charlie was just finishing his breakfast when Henry knocked lightly on the cabin door.

"Come in," said Sarah.

"Good morning, crew! Happy Fourth of July!" Henry greeted.

Charlie squealed with delight from his highchair.

"We're almost ready," said Sarah.

"That's good," said Henry, "because we don't want to be late."

Sarah looked at Henry with a funny expression. "What in the world could we possibly be late for at this time of day?" she thought.

Henry coaxed Charlie to eat the last of his eggs and to drink his milk. Sarah scurried about the cabin getting the last few things in order.

"I'll put his wagon and car seat in my truck," Henry said. "You two come out when you're ready."

Sarah and Charlie were only a few steps behind Henry. Storm sat and watched from the porch, which was now free of its plastic enclosure and screen door for the summer. Once the truck was out of view, he lay down on his bed and fell asleep.

Henry turned right instead of left out of the driveway. "Where are we going?" Sarah asked.

"You'll see," replied Henry.

It wasn't long before they turned into the narrow road that led to The Lodge. Sarah sat quiet. She certainly didn't mind coming here, but could not figure out why in the world they would be here at this hour.

Henry drove the truck past the house and down to the lake. "Let's go!" he said and hopped out of the truck before Sarah could respond. He opened her door and shined a flashlight so Sarah could see as she took Charlie out of the car seat and handed him to Henry. With Charlie and the flashlight in one arm, Henry held Sarah's hand as she stepped out of the truck.

"Right this way." He led them to the bench near the lake. "Ahhh..." he said, "now we just sit and watch."

Sarah smiled. "The sunrise? So that's what you're up to!"

Charlie snuggled up close to Henry. He was still a bit sleepy. Henry wrapped his arm around him to ward off the morning chill. His other arm was extended across the back of the bench and around Sarah. She laid her head on Henry's shoulder and they watched quietly as the sun made its appearance for the day.

"I couldn't imagine living somewhere without this luxury each day," Sarah commented.

"You're twice rewarded here, because when you sit on that bench over there," he shined the flashlight to another bench to the left, "you get to see the sun go down. We'll have to watch it sometime."

"I'd like that," said Sarah.

They watched until the sun had completely risen above the tree line. The morning was brightening quickly. Henry stood up, holding Charlie in one arm. "Come on, I want to show you something." He pulled on Sarah's hand, encouraging her up from the bench. She looked at The Lodge as they walked past the truck and up the hill.

"Henry Jacobson! You fixed the roof!"

Henry smiled and kept walking. As they approached the porch, he pulled a key from his pocket and unlocked the door.

Sarah looked around. "It's no longer boarded up!"

"Come on in," said Henry.

Sarah stepped into the large, log home. Though it wasn't exactly as she had pictured it in her mind, it was still impressive. The large stone fireplace was the first thing that caught her eye as she looked around. Henry lit a couple of the wall-mounted lanterns and began the tour.

To the right of the great room with the fireplace were two small bedrooms. Each had a double bed, a dresser, and a small potbelly woodstove.

The fireplace was just off center of the room. Behind it was a stairway that led upstairs to the loft that housed several beds, a couple of large trunks, and two dressers.

Sarah looked out one of the dormer windows, "This is just amazing, Henry."

"There's more," he said. "C'mon."

The trio went back down the steps, which were made of long logs that had been sliced in half. At the bottom of the stairway was a door that led outside. Henry brought Sarah to the kitchen. It had many windows and was very bright for a log home. Sarah stopped and looked around. "My! Look at that cook stove! It's huge! And this table and chairs!" She looked at the floor, "Where is the cellar? There it is!" she answered her own question.

Charlie was now walking around. He pointed to the woodstove and said, "Hot! Hot!"

"That's right, Charlie," Henry said. He was nearly laughing because Sarah seemed to overlook what he thought was one of the better features of the kitchen – the indoor sink.

She opened a door that was near the cellar door in the floor. It was dark inside, but she could tell it was a pantry. Beside it was another type of door. Its handle was at the top. "What's this?" asked Sarah.

Henry was right behind her. "Careful there." He pulled on the handle and slowly lowered what looked to be a long trunk.

Once all the way down, Sarah recognized it for what it was. "A bathtub!" she exclaimed.

The wooden case was lined with a smooth metal surface. Sarah stood and admired it. She thought of how it was such a chore for her to bathe. For Charlie it wasn't so bad, as she'd just set him in a large roaster pan. For her, it just wasn't quite as easy.

Henry lifted the tub back into the wall.

Then she spotted it. "A sink! With a pump!" she started to pump the short handle. Soon water began to trickle into the square basin and out the hole in the bottom. She let the pump handle down and pulled the curtain beneath the sink aside to reveal the five gallon bucket that the water drained into. Smiling, and admiring the kitchen as a whole, she looked at Henry. "You've been busy, haven't you?"

Henry smiled, "I just noticed that the roof needed fixing and it sort of snowballed from there. I didn't want the place to deteriorate."

Sarah walked into the great room and sat in an overstuffed chair near the fireplace. Charlie toddled behind her and tried to climb up into a chair opposite her. The chair had a sturdy wooden frame with wide armrests. Thick removable cushions covered the seat and the back. It was too tall for Charlie to climb, but Henry picked him up and sat him in it. The boy looked small.

"I just wanted to show you this house before we went to town for the fair," Henry explained. He sensed that Sarah was confused by his efforts. Only now did he doubt his approach to his surprise. He saw the added conveniences of this property to be so beneficial, but maybe it was too forward to think that Sarah would want them over her own small log home.

"You did a wonderful job, Henry. I don't know what the state of it was before you began, but I do know that it didn't look like this," Sarah smiled. Noticing Henry's quietness, she stood up and took his hand, "Henry, I do appreciate all of this, and I'd love to live here, but I'm just afraid that it will be too much for me to maintain. Just to heat it, well, that is a lot of wood to split."

"Yes, I guess I didn't think of that aspect," said Henry, even though he had. He also knew that she only knew of half of his plans. "But you could come and enjoy it throughout the summer, and eventually ol' Chuck here will be splitting the wood!"

Sarah laughed, "Oh, Henry! You're making him grow up so fast! However, I do think that would be an excellent job for him, eventually."

"Let's go," said Henry, relieved that any tension that may have existed was smoothed. "I have to get the horses over to the fairgrounds."

43

Even though it was barely seven o'clock in the morning, the fairgrounds were bustling with activity. Henry's truck and trailer were parked roughly in the same spot as last year. Sarah brushed the horses' shiny coats while Charlie played with some toys in the bed of the pickup. Henry was overseeing the eight to ten year olds who were decorating the hay wagon. It was going to be a beautiful day: sunny, but not too hot, and just a slight cool breeze every now and then.

Not far away, a bus filled with band members parked. The students filed out and were walking to the church.

"Time for breakfast!" Henry announced. He took Charlie out of the pickup bed and set him in the wagon. Sarah grabbed her backpack from the cab and put it in the wagon with Charlie.

The ladies of the church always made a pancake breakfast for those who volunteered their time to work the fair. Sarah learned that Charlie loved pancakes! "I'll have to make these for him," she said.

"I doubt you'd get complaints," replied Henry.

Charlie didn't say anything. He just watched the fork in Sarah's hand and held his mouth open for another bite.

The basement of the church was packed. As soon as people finished their breakfast and left, there would always be more people ready to take their seats. This was a no-nonsense, eat-and-get-back-to-work affair.

When they had finished, Sarah brought Charlie into the restroom to wash him up. She set him on the counter next to a sink and was cleaning the sticky boy with wet paper towels when Darla Taylor walked in.

"Good morning," greeted Sarah.

"I suppose it is," said Darla, not looking at Sarah or Charlie, but instead at her own reflection in the mirror.

Sarah left it at that and walked out of the restroom. Darla continued to fuss with her curls and makeup, seething with jealousy. "Good morning," she sneered to herself, trying to make a mockery of Sarah, once the restroom door shut.

Sarah found Henry waiting outside by Charlie's wagon. "I have to go hitch up the team and get everyone together on the wagon," he said. "The parade starts in an hour. You two can come along, or just hang out here."

"I think we'll hang out here, Henry. It will be easier to keep Charlie entertained. I'm going to bring him over to the playground by the school and let him run off some energy."

"Great idea!" Henry leaned down and kissed Sarah on the cheek. "Get some front row seats for the parade. I'll watch for you."

44

There was one other mother with her child at the playground. She had a little boy who was just about Charlie's age. The two boys played with each other, picking up the tiny pebbles that lined the play area and letting them fall through their fingers. The two young mothers chatted about their children and the festival in general.

Her name was Jenny, and her son's name was Billy. They weren't from this area. She and her husband came up north every Fourth of July to visit her grandparents and to go to the parade. Her husband was out fishing, but would be joining them soon.

When Jenny asked Sarah about her husband, all Sarah said was that he had passed away. She didn't provide any details, and Jenny didn't ask for any. She simply told her that she was sorry to hear that, and it was left at that. Sarah was glad. While Cory's fate saddened her, it was not something that she was going to grieve over for the rest of her life. Instead, she had decided to only remember the happy times they had together. She had to, for Charlie's sake. He had never met his father and he needed a mother who was strong. Sarah also knew that Cory would have wanted her to move on with life just as she was doing.

"It was nice to meet you, Sarah," said Jenny as she put Billy into his stroller.

"You too, Jenny. Perhaps we'll see each other next year," Sarah smiled. She scooped up Charlie and sat on a swing with him as they watched Jenny and Billy leave.

Charlie giggled as they went back and forth on the swing. "Is that fun, Charlie? Do you want to go a little higher?"

"How about a push?" a voice came from behind her.

Sarah stiffened as she felt a hand on her back pushing her and Charlie higher. She tightened her grip on Charlie and reached her feet toward the ground to stop the swing.

"Stop that!" said Sarah.

Bob McCarthy stepped in front of the swing and grabbed the chains. "Oh, do you want to stop?" he asked.

"Go away," said Sarah, looking around. The playground was behind the school, opposite of where the festival was being held. Jenny and Billy were gone and there was nobody in sight. Sarah ducked underneath Bob's arm and began to walk away with Charlie held close in her arms. Bob chased after her and grabbed one of her arms just above the elbow. Sarah started to run and yelled loudly, "Leave us alone!" She knew that they at least were in earshot of somebody and was hoping that her yelling would scare him off.

He did release his grip and Sarah continued to run toward the church, leaving the wagon and her backpack behind.

"Boy, some people just aren't the friendly type," Bob McCarthy said to himself, laughing as he walked in the opposite direction.

Sarah sat in the shade with Charlie to catch her breath. Her face was flushed. She looked at

Charlie who was looking at his mother with an expression that she had never seen before.

"Hidey! Hidey!"

Sarah turned and tried to compose herself, but Hank knew immediately that something wasn't right.

"What's the matter?" he asked.

"Oh, nothing, really. Just a playground bully," Sarah said.

"What are you talking about?"

Sarah told Hank of what had occurred and he knew by the description that it was Bob McCarthy she was talking about. "The boy has been trouble since diaperhood," said Hank. "You steer clear of him."

"Oh, I intend to," said Sarah.

"C'mon. I'll walk back with you to get your wagon."

Hank walked with Sarah and Charlie. He didn't want to alarm Sarah, but he also didn't want her to let her guard down where Bob McCarthy was concerned. He would speak with Al, and old time friend and the local sheriff. Al Doyle was all too familiar with Robert McCarthy. He never did anything to get locked up, but was always a breath away from it.

45

Hank, Sarah, and Charlie found a place on the parade route and sat down. John and Clare, then eventually Big Jake and Grace, joined them. The group visited and laughed as they waited for the parade to pass them. It wasn't long before they could hear the band in the distance. Just as he had last year, Henry led the parade with Suzie and Elaine pulling the wagon. This year, instead of Uncle Sam, there were four kids arranged underneath a gray sheet made to look like Mount Rushmore. It was a hit with the crowd.

The family waved to Henry as he drove the team past them. Henry tipped his hat and smiled. Other parade floats, clowns, and the band followed. As the end of the parade passed, the crowd broke up and headed for the games, rides, and food.

"We're going to go help Henry with the horses," Big Jake said. "We'll catch up with you ladies in a bit."

"Okay!" said Grace, before Sarah could respond. She had planned to go back to the truck too, but went along with Grace and Clare.

"There is Gerty! Oh, let's show Charlie to her. She'll love it!" Grace said as she walked over to a woman sitting on a bench. Sarah and the wagon were not far behind. "Gerty, this is Sarah and her son, Charlie."

Gerty looked up at Sarah. "Pleased to meet you," she said. Gerty was on old woman who was dressed in a long skirt and long-sleeved shirt. She had a scarf on her head and a shawl around her shoulders.

"Gerty is Lone Pine's most cherished resident. She has lived here for 101 years!" Clare said.

"It's a pleasure to meet you, Ma'am," said Sarah. "I suppose Charlie is among one of the youngest residents." She pulled the wagon closer.

Gerty let out a sweet giggle. "You look like you'll be a strapping young lad," she said, reaching a crooked hand out and letting Charlie hold on to one of her fingers.

"Sarah and Charlie are Brennys, Gerty. They are living on Lake Serene!" chirped Grace.

Gerty's blue eyes sparkled from behind her glasses. "Well, I'll be! You come from good lines, young lady. Keep it up! I knew your family well, I'm glad to see someone came back to set their roots. I worried that the younger generation would end up selling out."

"Oh, I have no intention of that, Ma'am," said Sarah without hesitation.

"Please, call me Gerty. And it was a pleasure to meet you, Sarah. And you too, Charlie. Heh-heh! Wait until you learn about who you were named after, little boy! I'm going to play some bingo now." Gerty stood up slowly with the aid of an old cane and shuffled away at a pace that was pretty good for a woman her age. Sarah could only imagine the stories that Gerty had to tell.

46

The men caught up with the women after about an hour. "Well," said Hank, "I've entered the meat raffle again. Do you suppose I'll ever win?"

"It might be your lucky year," said John, "but don't hold your breath."

"You know, Dad, you could have bought all that meat by now…" started Big Jake.

Hank held his hand up, "Don't ruin my fun, Sam. I've thought of that too, anyway. I think of it 'bout once a year. Heh-heh!"

"All right. I won't. But remember, you've always told us not to try to outwit our common sense," Big Jake concluded.

Sarah thought they were wise words of advice.

"Let's get something to eat," suggested Henry.

Sarah agreed. Charlie was getting very tired, but she wanted him to eat before he napped.

The group found themselves a picnic table and had a lunch of hotdogs and root beer. Charlie loved the hotdog. Sarah broke a few pieces off for him to chew on and he ate them eagerly. She let him try the root beer, but the bubbles startled him. She got him some water to drink instead. They talked about past fairs and shared funny stories, such as the time Henry ran back to his father's truck for his real fishing pole and tried to use it a the children's "fishing booth" game.

Henry said in his defense, "It's not like I put a worm on the hook, I'm not a fool. I used a jig. And I did catch a prize, but they disqualified me."

The group laughed. It was the mental image that made Sarah laugh.

"Oh, Sarah," Grace observed. "It looks like Charlie is ready for his nap."

The little boy was sitting on Sarah's lap, leaning back against her chest. She couldn't see his face, but she felt his head bob down every now and then.

Clare, who was sitting next to Sarah, said, "Here, let me make a nest for him in his wagon. He'll rest well in there." Clare folded a quilt to make a plush lining for Charlie to lie on. Sarah gently laid him down and covered him with a light blanket. He barely moved.

"Sarah, let's go for a ride on the Ferris wheel," Henry suggested. "Mom, will you keep an eye on Charlie for a little bit?"

"Of course I will!" Grace said quickly. "You two take your time. I have nowhere to go."

Sarah figured that Charlie would be little or no trouble, and she knew he was in good hands.

"Thanks!" Henry pulled Sarah's hand. "C'mon, let's go!"

Sarah went along willingly and was excited to see her property from the height of the Ferris wheel. The couple got in line and watched it go around until it was their turn to board. Henry handed the tickets to the boy at the gate. It was the same boy as last year, Sarah noticed. Henry held her hand and she stepped up into the chair, then he slid in behind her.

They were the last couple to be seated for this ride, so once they sat down the wheel began to go around continuously. Like last year, Henry pointed out things of interest. Sarah noticed that he seemed a little more excited than usual, but just thought he was having a good time. Eventually, the ride slowed down and the man operating the wheel unloaded the seats one by one. As their chair neared the top of the wheel, Henry pulled something out of his shirt pocket. He turned to Sarah, took a hold of her left hand and said, "Sarah, I love you. I want to spend the rest of my life with you. I love Charlie, too, and I want us to be a family. Sarah, will you marry me?"

Sarah looked down as he slid a pretty engagement ring on her finger. She looked up at Henry's eyes. They shined so blue at that moment, and her own eyes welled up with tears.

"Oh, Henry!" she said softly in his ear as she hugged him tightly. "Yes! Yes! I will marry you!"

Henry's heart pounded hard in his chest. Even though he had a good feeling that she would accept his proposal, he felt great relief when he actually heard her say "yes." They held each other tight and hadn't even noticed the movement of the Ferris wheel.

"Okay, you two, time to get off," the man said, unlocking their safety bar.

Sarah giggled and Henry lifted her out of the ride. They hurried back to the picnic table.

The newly engaged couple stood at the end of the table. "Everyone, I have an announcement to make. Sarah and I are getting married!" Henry proclaimed.

Henry's dad stood tall and proud with his hands on Grace's shoulders. Grace cried with happiness. Clare welled up, too. John shook Henry's hand and kissed Sarah on the cheek.

Then Sarah looked at Hank, the patriarch. Her eyes glowed with warmth and love. It was this man that made such a change in her life. She did not even want to think about how her life would be had his chickens never have gotten out at Carson's Spring. Sarah walked over to him and Hank stood up. They hugged and Hank whispered, "Welcome to our family, Sarah. We're proud to have you."

"Thank you, Hank. Thank you," she replied. Then she pulled back and looked at him. "Hank, will you give me away at the wedding?"

"'Course I will, Sarah. 'Course I will."

47

The young couple hadn't wasted any time. They were married the same summer that they became engaged. It was a small ceremony at St. Joseph's church with the reception held right there in the church basement. To some, it may have been far too simple of a wedding, but to the newlyweds, they wouldn't have had it any other way. They were celebrating with those they loved most, and any of the townspeople that wanted to join in the ceremony were welcome to come. Even Gerty made it.

The only way it could have been more perfect was if Sarah's mother had been there. Henry knew this was hard for Sarah, but admired how she handled it with such strength. Sarah knew in her heart, and her mind, that her mother would never expect her to just sit in that log cabin and wait for her. She knew that she was doing exactly what her mother wanted her to do – enjoy her life and move on with it.

After a few hours, the party began to fade, as did Charlie. He was sitting on Beth's lap, sleeping. Sarah crouched down beside Beth. "Shall I take him?" she asked.

Beth smiled, "If you must. It's fun to hold him when he's so content."

"Thanks for keeping an eye on him, Beth."

"You're welcome." Beth paused, then she said, "Sarah, congratulations. You're not so bad, after all."

"Thanks, Beth." Sarah smiled. She knew that coming from Beth, it was meant as a compliment.

Henry walked up behind Sarah, put his hand on her shoulder, kissed Charlie's sleeping head, and said quietly in her ear, "Let's go."

He led her away from the remainder of the crowd. They stopped and turned around. "Everyone!" Henry said above the chattering crowd. Mouths shut and heads turned. "Thank you for joining us today, it means a lot to us."

Everybody clapped and cheered as Mr. and Mrs. Henry Jacobson walked out of the room.

Henry turned the truck off. Sarah hadn't said anything when he drove past the cabin and headed right to The Lodge. "You wait here, I'll be right back," he said quietly to Sarah. He unfastened Charlie and carried him into the house.

Sarah leaned her head against the back of the truck seat. She thought of how wonderful this whole day had been, and how exciting her life was about to become.

Henry returned and scooped her out of the truck. He carried her up the porch steps and through the doorway.

"Honey, we're home."

To be continued...

About the Author

Nancy Ann resides in Minnesota, where she was born and raised. Annual family vacations to Northern Minnesota helped to inspire this book, as did her own personal lifestyle and many interests – among them, gardening, husbandry, and writing.

It was in December 2006, after giving birth to her 5th child, that she decided to put aside some of her petty hobbies such as sewing and crocheting and finally jot down the book that has been lingering in her head for over 25 years.

Other projects by IrisBlu Publishing:

Gym Rats children's book series
By Mary Reiss

Written for gymnasts, by a gymnast. Former NCAA gymnast and club coach, Mary Reiss, is the author of this fictional book series. It is ideal for girls from the beginning levels and pre-team on up through compulsories. Older and more advanced gymnasts will find the coaching tips and drills useful.

Book 1: *Basic Training*
Book 2: *Toe Jam*

With All Due Respect

Do you know an older American with a great story? IrisBlu Publishing is collecting the stories of our older Americans to be published in magazine form. These stories should be written by Americans 70 years of age or older and should capture what life was like in the early decades of the 20th Century. Please contact us for more information.

Transplant Stories

IrisBluPublishing is collecting stories, memoirs and personal essays from those people whose lives have been touched by organ donation and transplantation. Please contact us for more information.

www.IrisBluPublishing.com